Design Annual 2000

Design Annual 2000

Design Annual 2000

The International Annual of Design and Illustration
Das internationale Jahrbuch über Design und Illustration
Le répertoire international du design et de l'illustration

Publisher and Creative Director: B. Martin Pedersen

Editor: Chelsey Johnson Associate Editors: Heinke Jenssen, Nicole Ray

Art Director: Massimo Acanfora
Production: Dana Shimizu Photographer: Alfredo Parraga

Published by Graphis Inc.

(opposite) Lorenc Design (following page) Rolf Jansson (page 6) The Rocket Scientists (page 8) Peter Krämer

Contents Inhalt Sommaire

Remarks: We extend our heartfelt thanks to contributors throughout the world who have made it possible to publish a wide and international spectrum of the best work in the field of design. Entry instructions for all Graphis Books may be requested from: Graphis Inc., 141 Lexington Avenue, New York, NY 10016-8193 or visit our Web site, www.graphis.com

Anmerkungen: Unser Dank gilt den Einsendern aus aller Welt, die es uns durch ihre Beiträge ermøglicht haben, ein breites, internationales Specktrum der besten Arbeiten zu veröffentlichen. Teilnahmebedingungen für die Graphis-Bücher sind erhältlich bei: Graphis Inc., 141 Lexington Avenue, New York, NY 10016-8193. Besuchen Sie uns im World Wide Web, www.graphis.com

Remerciements: Nous remercions les participants du monde entier qui ont rendu possible la publication de cet ouvrage offrant un panorama complet des meilleurs travaux. Les modalités d'inscription peuvent être obtenues auprès de: Graphis Inc., 141 Lexington Avenue, New York, NY 10016-8193. Rendez-nous visite sur notre site web: www.graphis.com

THE ROCKET SCIENTISTS

Commentary **Kommentar** Commentaire

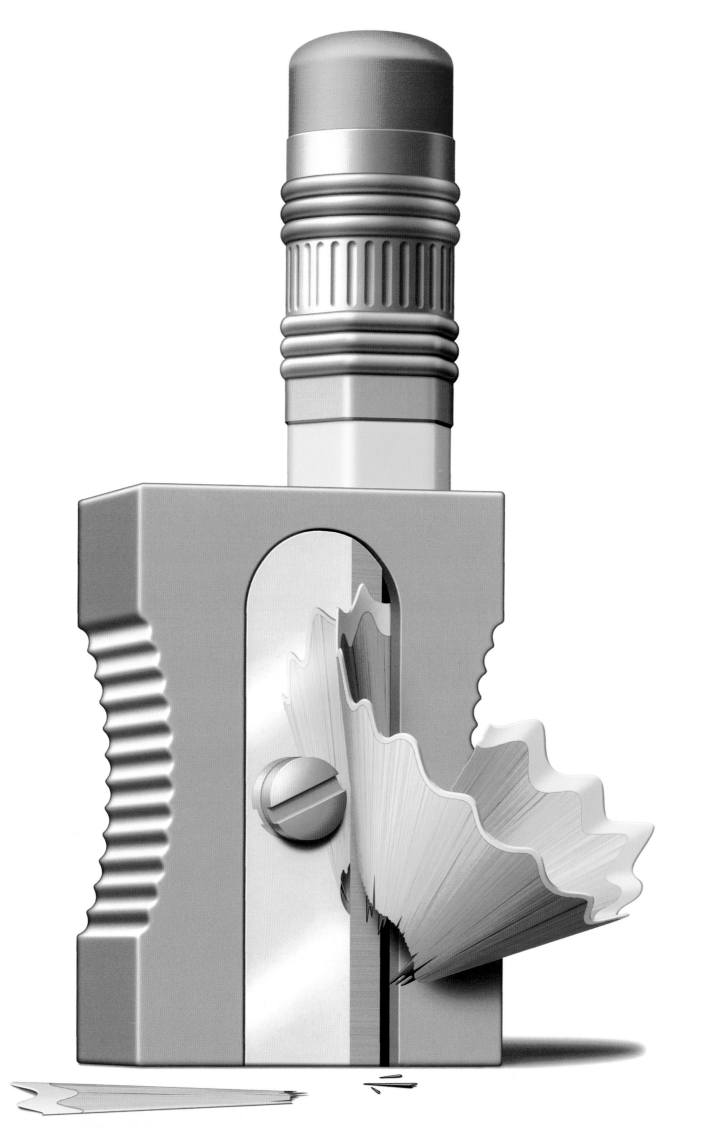

The Future of Design: A Creative Symposium

Apocalyptic and ordinary, thrilling and mundane, anticipated and dreaded, the click of the second that will begin the year 2000 has already begun to resonate through the way we view our world. For those in the design world, it's a crucial moment: Will design become a craft where technology presides over artistic impulse, or will the tenets of classic design hold steadfast as the waves of trends rise, crash, and ebb? To start off this Design Annual—the first of the new millennium—Graphis posed a question to several top designers from around the world: What is the future of design? Their responses, whether playful or serious, brief or extensive, exhibit an array of opinions as unique and diverse as their work.

If the twentieth century can be said to have faced a problem, it was without question the problem of speed. Speed has limits, and we spent the century finding and testing them. The blitzkrieg, the autobahn, the Olympics, Formula One, the sound barrier, the speed of light, of manufacture, of communication: all these accelerations generated quantities on a scale the world had never seen. Speed has worked its way into every facet of design experience. Its visual codes of seamless, sleek, aerodynamic surfaces and precarious balances have shaped our social and physical environments—such that everything from the blender to the Concorde to Little Boy to the Bullet Train to CNN is measured by its velocity.

As we enter the 21st century, I believe that the new problem facing us will be growth. In different ways, we (both as designers and global citizens) will need to broach this problem and test the limits of growth.

Growth, as I see it, is a problem separate from "speed" and "more" and "reproduction." It is time-based event, with breaking points and moments of rupture that generate entirely new conditions. In other words, growth is non-linear and unpredictable. I feel that this is important to emphasize. Many of us have come to see growth as an uninterrupted telos of progress. Few of us are ready to admit that growth is constantly shadowed by its constituitive opposite, that it is equal partners with death.

Immersed in the logic of growth, we have, for the most part, denied the liberating potential of death. (For us, there is only addition, never subtraction; permanence, never decay.) In our shortsightedness, we have banished death both from nature and from our approach to design practice. We seem unable to let go of even obvious corpses—first in the name of quality, then history, then nostalgia. Even second-rate substance is inflated with significance. Like taxidermists, we preserve the skin, and stuff the remains with modern infrastructure. The result is deeply inauthentic.

If we look at how growth behaves in nature, we see it coupled with a phenomenon of clearing. Forest fires produce a cycle of life and regeneration. Spring follows the barrenness of winter. Death opens up fields of potential.

I increasingly believe that the future of design rests in our ability and willingness to develop new practices and theories of form which are inextricably linked to, and informed by, life and growth. As we observe the life of the object, and the effect of that object on the life around it, we may learn that growth is not about limits in the same way that speed was because growth is about qualities, not quantities. More precisely, it is about the qualities—wild and incalculable—that emerge from quantities.

BRUCE MAU, *Toronto*

I am not a futurist. I like the present time more than the future. I cannot see clearly what graphic design will be in the next ten years, even less what will happen in the next century. I can only have hope. Of course, I see technology going very fast. It opens up new ways to design. It brings a new attitude towards creation. Poster design (which is what I like the most) will probably not exist anymore—most of the graphic design work will be done for television or Internet. The screen will be the "new poster" with animation, virtuality, interactivity and unlimited colors. The concept of ephemerality increase. Everything will be seen very fast, and of course will have to be done faster and faster. It might happen that graphic designers will not have any more time for thinking, for imagining, or for creating, because the production of the work will have to be done very quickly—just producing.

Yet at the same time that technology changes the way of working, the mentality of people evolves very slowly. We leave little room for invention in art. Money, business, fashion and power are the only criteria of success. Clients become more conservative, as every little change makes people afraid that they are more and more susceptible. I hope more freedom will be given to graphic designers to express themselves. Graphic design should be recognized as any other form of art, which is not the case nowadays, compared to architecture or furniture design. Does modernity still exist? Will it survive?

PHILIPPE APELOIG, *Paris*

As the end of the century draws near, graphic design has also begun a great transformation. High technology, beginning with the computer, has permeated the domain of the individual, and it has come to the point where even daily tasks can be completed only within the scope of these technologies. The Internet and e-mail are readily used for information exchange, of course, and now even for the purchase of ordinary goods. For people in my generation, recalling the post-war days of poverty, when the market sprang from the physical exchange of goods, it seems like another world. All this changed in the span of just 50 years. This wavering of values has not been just a matter of hardware; it has reached expression itself.

Take, as a familiar example, a letter. Since the '90s, letters have turned into faxes and e-mail. Faxes are exceedingly convenient. They come directly into the room, just like that. Even letters concerning extremely important matters make their one-sided, naked way onto the desk, where they lay scattered. Thanks to the fax, information can now be imparted immediately, but the sense of quality of the expression, and the material on which it arrives, is remarkably scanty. The meaning may come across, but one's feelings toward the recipient attain only meager expression. Even when the content of the fax is something that's quite important to the relationship between the people concerned, the flimsy piece of paper on which it arrives is readily crumpled and tossed straight into the wastebasket.

A letter is just one example, but graphic design has also been affected by this daily pattern, and the warmth of graphic expression has been lost. The sense of existence held by the reproductions of the Bible, or Japanese ukiyo-e woodblock prints, has been lost. With expressions in which only the meaning is the basis of information, those that like the fax, are transmitted electronically and printed out at the receiving end, it is not only the sense of quality, but the soul of the expression that is forfeited. "Making the mass-produced beautiful" was the idea at the origin of the Bauhaus movement, and is one way of thinking about communication in which the heart or soul is affected by the sense of touch. This is being crushed by the efficiency of the new media. There is no doubt that design has entered the age of meaning, as opposed to touch and form.

Not long ago, I made a corporate identity presentation to a certain company. However, there was a change in the company's business situation, and the necessity arose to append the C.I. The project returned to my office. When I opened the package, I was terribly surprised; the visual additions to the C.I. had already been made. Not only that, but the logo I'd designed had been perfectly copied and included in the final product.

When I asked, "Who redesigned this?", the man answered that it had been done by one of his subordinates. In an instant, my design sense and technique was lost. With a computer and the right software, anything can be done. Amateurs haven't received academic design education, and are more pliable in their ideas. Professional designers have been too insistent on the techniques and expressions of the past and have lost their freedom. There is apprehension that graphics is on its way from being a world of experts to being a world of amateurs.

I confine myself to Japanese design. There are a number of reasons for this, but the primary one is that I fear that the global standard for design is uniformity according to the ideology of efficiency. Today, no matter what airport at which you deboard, it's harder and harder to find design that gives you a sense of the atmosphere of the country. The joy of traveling is halved by the ubiquitous fluorescent ceilings, breakfasts of fried eggs and toast, and hamburger lunches.

One more thing. Lately, I have grown quite interested in the early to middle Edo era of the 17th and 18th centuries in Japan. There isn't another country in the world where peace has reigned for more than 250 years and the culture of the common person has so richly matured. Even the tying of a single cord

contains a wealth of design. Pottery and dyeing are rich in variations of technique and style. The plastic arts are simple, and the authorities of each era have exerted no pressure here. In a positive sense, these arts are both craftsmanlike and rational. Take kabuki and ukiyo-e; these arts have beautifully taken up the desires of the people. These are extremely 21st-century ideas, I think. On top of that, the lifestyle is simple and ecological. From the measure of the intellectual and magnificent Western culture, this is a difficult side to see. But what's more troubling is that most Japanese today have not realized this.

One of the themes of my work in the future will be to look at things one step removed from this "global standard."

IKKO TANAKA, *Tokyo*

You can design a piece of stationery and you can design your life. You can be an architect who creates a building or the architect for the foreign policy of a nation.

My use of the two words is similar. I believe in the *design of understanding* and in the *architecture of information*. I believe that the core of creative systemic work resides in the notion of learning.

So to more directly answer this query, the future of design will be dependent on design as the major facilitator for understanding—perhaps as the artistic guide/leader which will transform data into information, and encourage people to fly through an ether of understanding and select those things that form each of our personal pattern of clarity as we develop for our personal shelves of knowledge.

RICHARD SAUL WURMAN, *Newport, Rhode Island*

In the twenties, graphic design was one of the professions of the future. This was mainly caused by the great social engagement of the pioneers from that period: Russia, Bauhaus and the Netherlands. After World War II, though, graphic design became commercialized and eventually stopped being an interesting developing profession, because stylistic durability was nowhere to be found.

In the next century, the emphasis will be on human communication and intuition. Since women tend to exhibit both qualities more than men, graphic design is likely to become dominated by women. Already the number of female design students at art schools is much greater than twenty years ago, and in some situations there are more female than male students.

Graphic design is heading for a time of more depth and engagement again. Concepts like "stylistic durability" will return. In other words, it will be a time for design classics, in static as well as dynamic images.

This century the most vain people are opera singers, followed by ballet dancers, and after that graphic designers. In the next century, graphic designers will have disappeared from this list.

GERT DUMBAR, *The Netherlands*

In my view, the graphic design industry faces two crucial and immediate opportunities. For the last few decades Graphic Design has been treated as a poor second cousin by both the advertising and the broadcast TV Industries. There are many historical and economic reasons for this.

Even with the imminent arrival of the much anticipated "convergence" of computer, television, and broadband telecoms, both of these industries are still quite obviously struggling to come to terms with the languages, the information structures, the technologies, the economics, in short the sheer complexity of multi-linear, multi-dimensional, multi-platform, multi-audience interactive media. Both industries generate high revenues for what in essence always seems to equate to concise story-telling, whether that be soundbite, 15-second commercial, promo clip, or six-part mini-series. In a mediaspace where "stories" are not necessarily held in lower regard but are subsets of larger containers of media, and information as you need it, how you want it becomes the norm, navigation and interface become key, and audience inclusive strategies are required to maintain audience interest and involvement.

The graphic design profession has made significant inroads into understanding and developing solutions for interactive media, whilst both TV and advertising either scratch their heads or merely scratch the surface. The time is now for graphic design to seize those opportunities, seize those revenue streams, and generate true future media for a future generation.

MALCOLM GARRETT, *London*

As we enter a new decade, a new crop of passionate, talented, intuitive, designers will emerge to reclaim their profession (temporarily highjacked by a misguided few in the 90s.)

DAVID CARSON, *New York*

Whether we like it or not, the coming generation Y in the first century of the third millennium will look down on us and make fun of our relatively primitive media. Our beloved pets like the personal computer and the Internet, mobile phone and Notebook, will be exhibited in a media zoo as examples of a hyperactive society.

Handling the media will become a child's play, and this will contribute to a common illiteracy. Graphic designers will be as superfluous as nonsmokers, because once our clients will finally be able to speak with the computer, they won't need us anymore. The appropriate do-it-yourself software will include aesthetics programs which will automatically hit the nerve of mainstream society, and which will allow any small demolition expert to build his own nuclear bomb. On the other hand, the difference between Little Red Riding Hood and the wicked wolf will disappear just as the frogs disappeared from the data highway. To us, this "fabulous age" will be terribly boring.

UWE LOESCH, *Wuppertal, Germany*

Because of our easy access to technology today, more and more people will be experimenting with design. Almost anyone can do it, and it's becoming more universal. You will see less of single trends, and more of different types of designs going on at the same time. Because of this diversity, design will become much more personal.

Type and graphics in general will become more like imagery, which we have started to already see the last couple of years. You'll of course have the old guard who will continue to work with the classic typefaces, but you'll also see more and more of this new illegible, illustrative type. It's becoming less about reading, and more about feeling.

FABIEN BARON, *New York*

Design is influenced/swayed by the nature of the culture of the country of origin, which in turn depends on the economic situation and the people's sensibilities. It's therefore impossible to make a single sweeping statement about the future of design. What is clear is that the future of design is an age of high-speed,

"A technology-inspired 'NEW PERSON' is in the making, whose habitat is 'NEW CITY'—the cyber site on 'COMPUTER ISLAND,' part of a vast archipelago. Each island is occupied by one 'NEW PERSON,' who is not necessarily lonely. This person's ancestors could have been you or me."

high-efficiency creation, thanks to the computer.

I don't have the least anxiety or doubt concerning the computer age (and it will come). In my design work, I treasure the process leading up to completion; that's the part that's both enjoyable and important. I plan to continue creating "Fukuda-esque" design, design that only Fukuda can do. I am of the mind that thinking about the future of design is the same as thinking about myself.

SHIGEO FUKUDA, *Tokyo*

Graphic design is no longer about form and color but about process development. The demands on the profession have turned so complicated that traditional paradigm-oriented solutions no longer work.

Graphic design thinking knows only one structural integrated "knowledge-system"—functionalist design as developed in the second half of this century, when design moved from printed matter into the "real" world.

The rest is philosophy, mathematics, psychology, economy, law, and history. These building elements are not yet integrated into design thinking as they are in, for instance, architecture. Architects, when building a model, can judge this model on the basis of these elements. Architects will also build models without being asked by a client. Rem Koolhaas became in the eighties the most influential architect of this century on the basis of his models and not on the basis of his finished buildings.

Graphic design is desperately in need of an equivalent of this model-building. Client-propelled paradigms no longer hold against the needs of this changing world. Young graphic designers are aware of this and are looking to philosophy, mathematics, psychology, economy, law, and history to provide them with the elements to build models of design and accelerate progress in design-thinking. Anyway, I see my students doing exactly this, and as we all know, they *are* the future.

GERARD HADDERS, *The Netherlands*

In a world of as many realities as the number of its occupants, and other realities of a more collective nature, there now exists a virtual reality. A new form of communication is being established. A technology-inspired "NEW PERSON" is in the making, whose

"Will the language of design survive transfiguration? Naturally, the language of the present day cannot be expected to remain as it is. Finding a designer who thinks of design as something done with a pencil or brush will be harder than finding a seashell on a mountain."

"Amateurs haven't received academic design education and are more pliable in their ideas. Professional designers have been too insistent on the techniques and expressions of the past and have lost their freedom. Some fear that graphics is on its way from being a world of experts to being a world of amateurs."

"In our short-sighted-ness, we have banished death both from nature and from our approach to design practice. Even second-rate substance is inflated with significance. Like taxidermists, we preserve the skin, and stuff the remains with modern infrastructure. The result is deeply inauthentic."

habitat is "NEW CITY"—the cyber-site on "COMPUTER ISLAND." "NEW PERSON" commands numerous intelligence agents, possesses armies on every continent—and can master international communication, online.

"COMPUTER ISLAND" is part of a vast archipelago. Each island is occupied by one "NEW PERSON" who is not necessarily lonely. This person's ancestors could have been you or me. To maintain the communication with the rest of the archipelago, one is dependent on technological innovations and is adaptable to changes. "NEW PERSON" is now ready for an encounter with its infinite subconscious—virtual reality.

"NEW PERSON" acts through coded linear patterns, in systematic order, using graphic form infrastructure manipulated by a "NEW DESIGNER" whose arena is "DESIGNISM."

"DESIGNISM" is the practice of visualizing the human adaptation to changing technologies, in a quest for economic survival. "DESIGNISM" has no conflict with design as we know it, but rather depends on its visual, social, moral and philosophical values and heritage. Since it is possible that the occupant of "COMPUTER ISLAND" may never have been exposed to treasures of the past and humanistic thought, it may need guidance.

At the "CONTROL CENTERS," designers improve the flow of communication on the "COMPUTER ISLANDS" with seductive persuasion. They can effectively bring the "NEW PERSON" to its destinations, with human commitment towards its well-being. They can also point at ways leading nowhere, and can master the power to create chaos and total collapse of communication.

The "NEW DESIGNERS" in the "CONTROL CENTERS" are the bridging engineers of communication between human beings, as well as between the individual and the virtuality.

YAROM VARDIMON, *Tel-Aviv*

I love to explore. I love new ideas and challenges. I love quality. I love type. Univers, Frutiger, News Gothic, Bodoni, Sabon, Centennial, Walbaum, Garamond, Caslon, GST Polo, Rotis & Myriat. I love type designed by Adrian Frutiger, Ottl Aicher, David Quale and Matthew Carter. And I love spontaneous lettering by butchers, bakers, and news vendors. All that pretentious, amateurish, funky-punky crap created worldwide by so-called freaks I cannot stand—as a matter of fact, I hate it.

I am not referring to old or new, progressive or traditional. I'm talking about talent that becomes visible. I'm talking about consideration for people—even respecting and accepting the client's aspirations. I'm talking about politeness, respect, knowledge and hopefully elegance and timelessness. I love all people and designers who work hard at improving things to the benefit of mankind.

I hate layered, unreadable layouts. I feel sorry for clients who buy that kind of mediocrity from so-called designers, clients who let themselves be drowned in superfluous, non-commercial clutter! I feel sorry for people (young and old) who try desperately to be with it. I love talent, a positive outlook on life, and a liberal, generous attitude towards graphic design in particular. Garbage has the built-in property to rot away. It was like this yesterday, today, and (joy in my heart!) it will be like this tomorrow. Get my point, punk!

I thoroughly love my work—always did. And contrary to what you might think, I'm not frustrated, because I'm convinced my thinking will prevail.

FRITZ GOTTSCHALK, *Zürich*

The shape of the future of design depends on the span of the future in question. I'd like to consider the changes that will occur in the 100 years of the 21st century.

Will the language of design survive transfiguration? Naturally, the language of the present day cannot be expected to remain as it is. Perhaps an incredible new tool will arise to replace the computer, one that while maintaining the computer at the core of thinking, will overturn the very foundations of current values. And the passionate relationship between the computer and design will become a topic of the past.

The development of clones in the scientific world will repaint the real world in an absurd direction, and we will see the birth of clone designers. The standardization of design that transcends ages, races, and locales will accelerate. And the notion of hybrid design will be forgotten. The title of designer may even die out in time. Finding a designer who thinks of design as something done with a pencil or brush will be harder than finding a seashell on a mountain.

EIKO ISHIOKA, *Tokyo*

Design Annual 2000

1223735181
5460981026
3021425593
2760239114
1518962 0 3
6235145 4 1
3201049196
9110260352
2506925419

STRENGTH IN NUMBERS

Design Firm:
Slaughter Hanson
Art Director,
Designer: Marion
English Powers
Writer: Gary Brandon
Illustrator: David Webb
Photographers:
Don Harbor,
Fredrik Broden
Client: Greater
Alabama Boy Scout
Council

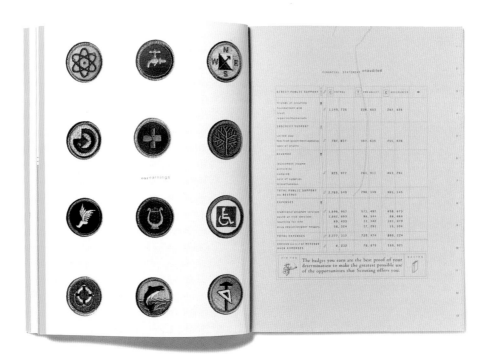

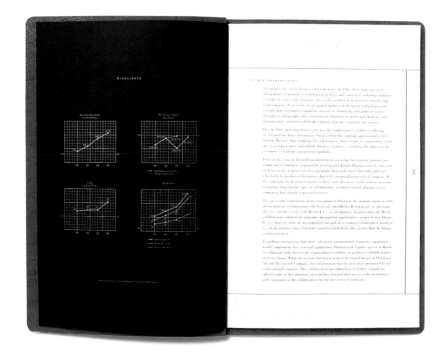

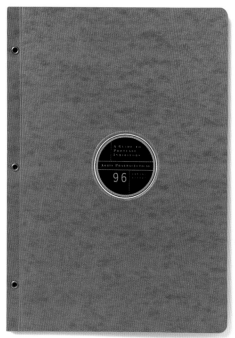

Design Firm:
Schulte Design
Creative Director,
Art Director,
Designer:
Paul Schulte
Writer: Arris
Pharmaceutical
Photographer:
Jim Karageorge
Client: Arris
Pharmaceutical

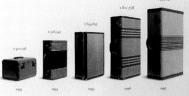

Design Firm:
Goodby Silverstein &
Partners Design
Creative Directors:
Rob Price, Paul Curtin
Art Director, Designer:
Keith Anderson
Writer: Michelle Bekey
Illustrator:
Keith Anderson
Photographer:
Bill Abronowicz
Client:
Williams Sonoma Inc.

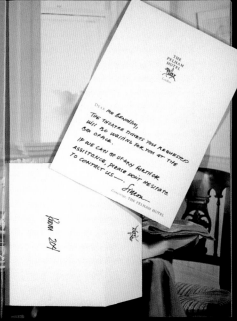

This is a business in which you either make tracks or follow them. In 1997, our company chose to make them.

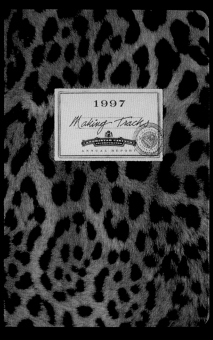

1997
Making Tracks
AMERISTAR CASINOS INCORPORATED
ANNUAL REPORT

Design Firm:
Goodby Silverstein &
Partners Design
Creative Directors:
Rob Price, Paul Curt
Art Director:
Paul Curtin
Designer: Clark Richard
Writer: Rob Price
Illustrator: Bob Conge
Photographer:
Bill Abronowicz
Client: Ameristar
Casinos Inc.

The following data has been derived from the audited financial statements of the Company and should be read in conjunction with those statements, certain of which are included in this Report.

INCOME STATEMENT DATA:	For the year ended 3/26/93	For the three mos. ended 12/31/93	For the year ended 12/31/94	For the year ended 12/31/95	For the year ended 12/31/96	For the year ended 12/31/97
(Amounts in thousands, except per share data)						
REVENUES:						
Casino	$ 20,285	$ 7,508	$ 90,882	$ 99,364	$161,336	$173,077
Food and beverage	10,154	2,521	17,404	19,302	34,250	36,672
Rooms	6,812	1,491	7,586	7,861	7,641	9,665
Other	8,747	1,317	7,822	7,796	7,789	8,273
	55,998	13,467	123,778	134,284	208,989	221,709
Less: Promotional allowances	4,982	1,208	9,420	10,417	12,824	15,530
Net revenues	50,926	12,158	114,393	123,867	188,465	206,179
COSTS AND EXPENSES:						
Casino	13,047	3,310	40,347	44,502	75,685	78,732
Food and beverage	6,758	1,922	12,469	11,747	16,773	20,784
Rooms	1,971	312	2,249	2,404	2,368	2,130
Other	8,005	1,391	8,412	8,211	7,054	7,546
Selling, general and administrative	10,070	2,712	28,492	29,197	47,758	51,358
Depreciation and amortization	4,185	993	7,062	9,721	14,135	16,358
Abandonment loss	—	—	—	—	—	646
Preopening costs	—	—	5,468	—	7,379	—
Total costs and expenses	42,146	10,640	104,492	105,782	171,152	178,155
INCOME FROM OPERATIONS	7,880	1,518	9,244	18,084	17,313	28,024
OTHER INCOME (EXPENSE):						
Interest income	43	9	86	205	354	445
Interest expense	(756)	(20)	(3,319)	(3,958)	(8,363)	(12,167)
Other	26	2	(5)	—	(77)	(38)
Income before income tax provision	7,199	1,509	6,646	14,331	9,287	16,327
Income tax provision	2,294	575	2,426	5,736	3,390	5,959
Income before extraordinary loss and cumulative effect of a change in accounting principle	4,905	925	4,220	9,995	5,897	10,368
Extraordinary loss on early retirement of debt, net of income tax benefit of $353 and $287, respectively	—	—	—	(637)	—	(672)
Cumulative effect of a change in accounting principle: Adoption of SFAS 109 "Accounting for Income Taxes"	—	720	—	—	—	—
NET INCOME	$ 4,905	$ 1,645	$ 4,220	$ 8,428	$ 5,897	$ 9,695

INCOME STATEMENT DATA:	For the year ended 3/26/93	For the three mos. ended 12/31/93	For the year ended 12/31/94	For the year ended 12/31/95	For the year ended 12/31/96	For the year ended 12/31/97
(Amounts in thousands, except per share data)						
PRO FORMA NET INCOME (unaudited):						
Income before pro forma income tax provision	$ 7,778					
Pro forma income tax provision	2,645					
Pro forma net income	$ 5,133					
EARNINGS PER SHARE:						
Income before extraordinary item						
Basic and diluted			$ 0.21	$ 0.45	$ 0.29	$ 0.51
Net income						
Basic and diluted			$ 0.21	$ 0.42	$ 0.29	$ 0.48
PRO FORMA EARNINGS PER SHARE (unaudited)	$ 0.27	$ 0.08				
WEIGHTED AVERAGE SHARES OUTSTANDING			20,260	20,260	20,260	20,260
PRO FORMA WEIGHTED AVERAGE SHARES OUTSTANDING	18,444	19,971				

BALANCE SHEET AND OTHER DATA:	as of 3/26/93	as of 12/31/93	as of 12/31/94	as of 12/31/95	as of 12/31/96	as of 12/31/97
Cash	$ 2,853	$ 3,160	$ 14,787	$ 10,724	$ 13,031	
Total assets	66,711	125,347	202,720	270,622	336,186	
Total notes payable and long-term debt, net of current maturities	34,686	45,200	101,809	142,892	193,112	
Stockholders' equity	26,844	56,690	65,847	78,914	81,626	
Capital expenditures	29,158	33,229	64,782	76,388	78,634	

Financial data as of dates and for periods ending prior to November 1993 reflect restated financial statements given retroactive effect to a corporate reorganization completed immediately prior to the closing of the Company's initial public offering. Pursuant to the reorganization, CPT and ACVI, then companies under the common control of Craig H. Neilsen, became wholly owned subsidiaries of the Company. In connection with this reorganization and the initial public offering, the Company elected to terminate its S corporation tax status effective January 1, 1993. Net income for the year ended September 30, 1993 includes a pro forma income tax provision using a rate of 34% to reflect the estimated income tax expense the Company would have incurred had it been subject to federal income taxes for the year.

The Vicksburg Casino and certain other portions of Ameristar Vicksburg opened in late February 1994. The remaining Ameristar Vicksburg facilities were completed and opened through May 1994. The Council Bluffs Casino opened in mid-January 1996. Portions of the land-based facilities at Ameristar Council Bluffs opened in June, November and December 1996. Ameristar Council Bluffs' remaining land-based facilities opened in February and March 1997.

No dividends were paid in 1994, 1995, 1996 and 1997. A $2.0 million dividend was paid to the Company's stockholder in September 1993 prior to the Company's conversion from a subchapter S corporation to a C corporation.

"This is our sixth year of reporting. We now know how much carbon dioxide our operations contribute to global warming. Similarly with hazardous wastes, ozone depleters and solvents: we have the data and we can see the trends. We have been able to set ourselves business-wide reduction targets in some key environmental impact areas and, in addition, local targets are widespread across all parts of the business. As we have progressed internally, the external view of what is needed has also moved forward. Previously environmental improvement was the goal, but now we must grapple with a more demanding objective – sustainability. It's not often I quote politicians but sustainability was neatly encapsulated as 'not cheating on your children'; that's the underlying motive for me. In a fast moving business like music, we will need to make a concerted effort to plan for these long term issues. I believe that there are already good business reasons for devoting attention to sustainability. We need to attract the best employees; to be in tune with customers and investors; to be the partner of choice for artists; and of course we need to use resources cost effectively. Particularly in an industry which has largely ignored the subject, we have an opportunity to demonstrate that EMI is genuinely exceptional and is taking the lead."

Sir Colin Southgate, Chairman

Energy crisis – is it for real?

IN THE '70s IT SEEMED WE WERE ON THE BRINK OF OIL RUNNING OUT. GAS GUZZLING CARS QUEUED AT PETROL STATIONS FOR RATIONED FUEL. BUT IT NEVER HAPPENED. IN THE '90s WE'RE MORE WORRIED ABOUT GLOBAL WARMING. SO IS THE THREAT REAL THIS TIME?

Scientists can't prove it for certain but the evidence is mounting that we do have a real problem. The people of the world are using more energy than ever before. Every litre of fuel burned means another cloud of carbon dioxide gas (CO_2) sent skywards.

The CO_2 is forming a blanket around the world and literally warming us up with the prospect of untold disruption to climate, rainfall and nature.

Politicians are worried as well – the Climate Change Conference in Kyoto, Japan, was held to agree a way forward. The result is a global treaty containing reduction targets for industrialised countries. We will all have to make savings if the targets are to be met – and business has got to find ways of making more products using less energy.

These images represent simulated and predicted changes in the earth's annual mean surface temperature, at 20 year intervals, from 1860 to 2050. (Reproduced courtesy of the UK Meteorological Office, Hadley Centre)

Environmental Report 1998 — The EMI Group

Targets and commitments 1997/98 and 1998/99 — The EMI Group

"This is our sixth year of reporting. We now know how much carbon dioxide our operations contribute to global warming. Similarly with hazardous wastes, ozone depleters and solvents: we have the data and we can see the trends. We have been able to set ourselves business-wide reduction targets in some key environmental impact areas and, in addition, local targets are widespread across all parts of the business. As we have progressed internally, the external view of what is needed has also moved forward. Previously environmental improvement was the goal, but now we must grapple with a more demanding objective – sustainability. It's not often I quote politicians but sustainability was neatly encapsulated as 'not cheating on your children'; that's the underlying motive for me. In a fast moving business like music, we will need to make a concerted effort to plan for these long term issues. I believe that there are already good business reasons for devoting attention to sustainability. We need to attract the best employees; to be in tune with customers and investors; to be the partner of choice for artists; and of course we need to use resources cost effectively. Particularly in an industry which has largely ignored the subject, we have an opportunity to demonstrate that EMI is genuinely exceptional and is taking the lead."

Sir Colin Southgate, Chairman

Contents

Chairman's statement
1   Thinking of the future
2   Energy crisis – is it for real?
6   Cleaning up our act at the factory
10 Local companies play their part
14 Creating an impact
18 Beyond our boundaries
    Targets and commitments (booklet at back)

and project management are located centrally in the Cellar on a Sun SPARC 1000 Ultra machine with 2 processors and 256 Mb RAM. The database system is Sybase 11.01. ➤ "We had a lot of problems in the beginning" says Morten Kopperud who is Computer Support Manager for Telenor R&D. "We started with AGRESSO in the autumn of 1995 and went into production on 1 January 1996. The Windows clients were new then and this produced some instability which required extra monitoring and attention from the IT department. In August 1996, we obtained a new version for the client and also stable server software. Since then the system has been stable and has worked well. This has significantly reduced the need for monitoring. But every database needs attention and we check daily with logs sent to the IT staff on duty." ➤ The computer department has responsibility centrally for 11 servers in the computer room and "some in the printer room". All operation is completely automatic. "This is modern network technology" says Kopperud. "The physical location of the servers is not important. The users work with their own screen at their own workplace – they don't need to know where the data comes from."

One year without a single stop – the extremely stable combination of AGRESSO and Sybase "It was exciting to see whether the system coped with more than 800 users on-line" says Kopperud. "We quickly discovered some bottlenecks. Some of these were caused by the transfer capacity of the network. Others were caused by the configuration of the system centrally. We increased the speed at several places in the network and together with Sybase we removed all the limitations. We have had good experiences with the system. The network is now correctly balanced and the combination of AGRESSO and Sybase is extremely stable and responsive. We have not had an unscheduled stop for well over a year. We appreciate not having problems."

When an organisation's business units are geographically dispersed, AGRESSO allows data to be analysed from remote locations instantly. Remote databases are polled by central servers on a user-defined time schedule or on demand.

(opposite)
Design Firm: Stocks Austin Sice
Creative Director,
Art Director, Designer:
Alan Delgado
Writer: EMI Group (in-house)
Photographers: Simon Fowler,
Max Jourdan
Client: EMI Group

(this page)
Design Firm: Bryce Bennett
Communications
Creative Director, Art Director,
Designer: Bryce Bennett
Illustrator: Rolf Jansson
Client: Agresso Group

Revenue NOK mil | Numbers of employees

155.0	97	225
73.8	96	113
44.1	95	71
20.3	94	50
22.9	93	40

Revenue per country

Norway 33%

Development costs NOK mil | Operating profit before R&D NOK mil

9.0	93	9.7
11.0	94	11.3
12.0	95	18.9
15.0	96	18.0
29.3	97	30.1

Report of the Board of Directors

Agresso Group ASA's international expansion continued at full speed in 1997. Higher growth targets than planned were achieved and turnover increased by 110 per cent compared with 1996 figures. The integration with Ampersand Systems Ltd was an important event in 1997. Comparable figures for 1996 on a pro forma basis have been made. All comparing figures for 1996 were nothing other as specified refers to the pro forma figures. The approximately NOK 82 million private placement carried out in August ensured the company a sound financial basis for its further expansion. The launch of version 5 in January 1997 represented an important step for the company and Agresso's products held a very good competitive position in the markets in which it operates. 62 per cent of its turnover took place outside Norway. As expected, the expansion negatively affected the 1997 result, as expansion costs have been charged to expenses as they were occurred.

Turnover and profit The group's operating revenues rose from NOK 73.8 million in the 1996 accounts to NOK 155 million in 1997, an increase of 110 per cent. Pro forma 1996 including Ampersand shows an income growth of 44 per cent. The increase in the AGRESSO activity was approximately 76 per cent from 1996. Product sales increased by 82 per cent based on the actual figures for 1996 and comprised 51 per cent of turnover, a decrease from 55 per cent in 1996. The product share has been weakened somewhat due to the merger with Ampersand. However the company's goal of having a high product share remains. Maintenance accounted for 17 per cent of the turnover, while consultancy services stood for 32 per cent.

The operating profit amounted to NOK 0.8 million, which is less than last year's profit of NOK 2.9 million. All the product and development costs have been charged to expenses as they were incurred. All the costs relating to expansion into new markets have also been charged as expenses. A weaker partner sale and non-recurring costs in connection with acquiring the customer liabilities from one of our former partners in Sweden have reduced the profit in 1997. This has resulted in the company not achieving the target for 1997 of 5-10 per cent profit margin before tax. Agresso's share (22%) of the profit of Engsoft is included with NOK 1 million.

The company's financial position is sound and its net financial items amounted to NOK 2.2 million in 1997. This contributed to the profit before tax amounting to NOK 3.1 million, compared with NOK 5.2 million in 1996. The profit after tax was NOK 2.8 million in 1997, as against NOK 3.2 million the year before.

Strategy Agresso's long-term goal is to be a significant international supplier of administrative software. The company has chosen to concentrate on software in the fields of finance, logistics, payroll/human resources and project management, which accounts for around 80 per cent of the total market for business software. Agresso has no ambition to supply production and materials administration systems itself. The marketing of AGRESSO in this market will take place through OEM agreements with existing players. An OEM agreement was entered into with Symix Systems Inc. in the USA in January, regarding the

(this page)
Design Firm: Fossil (in-house)
Creative Director, Art Director:
Tim Hale. Designers: Stephen Zhang,
Casey McGarr. Writer: Doug Helton
Illustrator: Patrick Reeves
Photographer: Rick Bryant, Blaine Leist
Client: Fossil

(opposite, top)
Design Firm: Sayles Graphic Design
Creative Director, Designer,
Illustrator: John Sayles
Writer: Annie Meacham
Client: American Cancer Society

(opposite, bottom)
Design Firm: O&J Design Inc.
Art Director, Designer:
Andrzej J. Olejniczak
Client: Avon Products Inc.

cream

10 curators — 10 writers — 100 artists

contemporary art in culture

PHAIDON

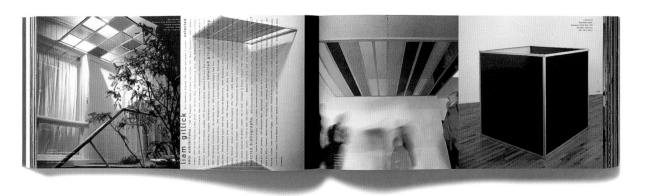

Design Firm:
Phaidon Press (in-house)
Art Director: Alan Fletcher
Designer: Julia Hasting
Client: Phaidon Press

(this page)
Design Firm: Factor Design
Creative Director: Johannes Erler
Art Director, Designer, Typographer:
Christian Tönsmann
Photographer: Frank Stöckel
Client: Hermann Schmidt Mainz

(opposite)
Design Firm: Dondina & Associati
Creative Director, Art Director,
Designer: Francesco Dondina
Photographer: Moreno Gentili
Client: Charta Book Editor

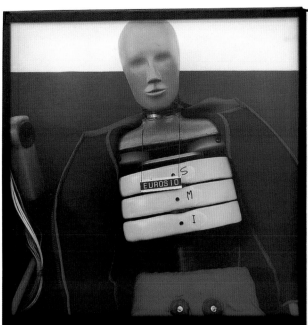

(this spread)
Design Firm: CFD Design
Creative Director: Mike Campbell
Designer: John Havel
Client: The Bellagio Gallery
of Fine Art

I BELIEVE THAT GREAT ART — WHETHER IN
PAINTING, SCULPTURE, ARCHITECTURE, MUSIC,
OR DANCE — HAS ALWAYS HAD THE POWER TO
DEEPLY STIMULATE HUMAN CONSCIOUSNESS...
I LOVE TO LOOK AT A LANDSCAPE BY CLAUDE
MONET. I FEEL ROMANTIC AND TRANSPORTED BY
A SCENE IN MONTMARTRE PAINTED BY AUGUSTE
RENOIR. I AM PROVOKED BY A PORTRAIT BY
PABLO PICASSO OR VINCENT VAN GOGH AND
DELIGHTED BY THE DANCING COLORS OF HENRI
MATISSE. I AM WARMED WHEN I AM NEAR THE
BLAZING CREATIVE HEAT OF JACKSON POLLOCK
OR WILLEM DE KOONING. THERE IS, FOR ME, A
PALPABLE ENERGY THAT RADIATES FROM THEIR
WORKS. ALL OF THESE ARTISTS, REGARDLESS OF
CHRONOLOGY, SHARE THE MOST REMARKABLE
POWER TO MOVE US. I FEEL THEM AND SOMEHOW
AM STIMULATED TO THINK AND FEEL MORE ABOUT
THE WORLD AROUND ME THAN I DID BEFORE.

STEPHEN A. WYNN

Orange Marilyn
ANDY WARHOL

Woman with Beret
PABLO PICASSO

Portrait of Paul Guillaume
AMEDEO MODIGLIANI

(this page)
Design Firm: Hans Sures
Designer, Photographer: Hans Sures

(opposite)
Design Firm: Commarts Design
Creative Director,
Art Director: Ian Newlands

Designers: Ian Newlands,
Alex Roberts
Writers: Mark Di Somma,
Patricia Capill
Illustrator: Ross Jones
Client: New Zealand Post Ltd.,
Stamp Business Unit

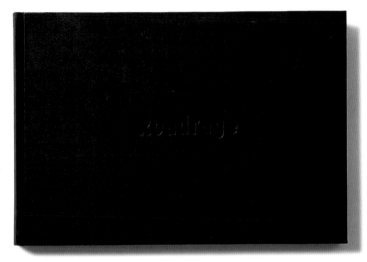

They all kept sliding in and out of focus, everybody moving
wavily as if the entire White Front had been moved underwater
somewhere off the Florida Keys. And little bits of conversation
drifted in and out of my head, sometimes hanging there for
a minute or two so I could study what was being said as though
it had been printed right on the smoke over our table:
"Will you get the hell up?
   Yer sitting on Stroker's cast, for chrissakes ..."
"Did you hear he was in the maternity ward?"
"... and Lugs knocked the fireman on his ass."
"... stole the ambulance." Throb.
Another round of beer here, Grace.
"What're you doing wrapped in a blanket, fella? You playing
   cowboys and Indians?"
"Who ast you? If that man wants to sit here in a blanket, it's
   fine, you follow me?"

Design Firm: Hirano Studio
Designer: Keiko Hirano
Design Assistant: Kanako Ooyanagi
Illustrator: Tamie Okuyama
Client: Okuyama Jimusho Inc.

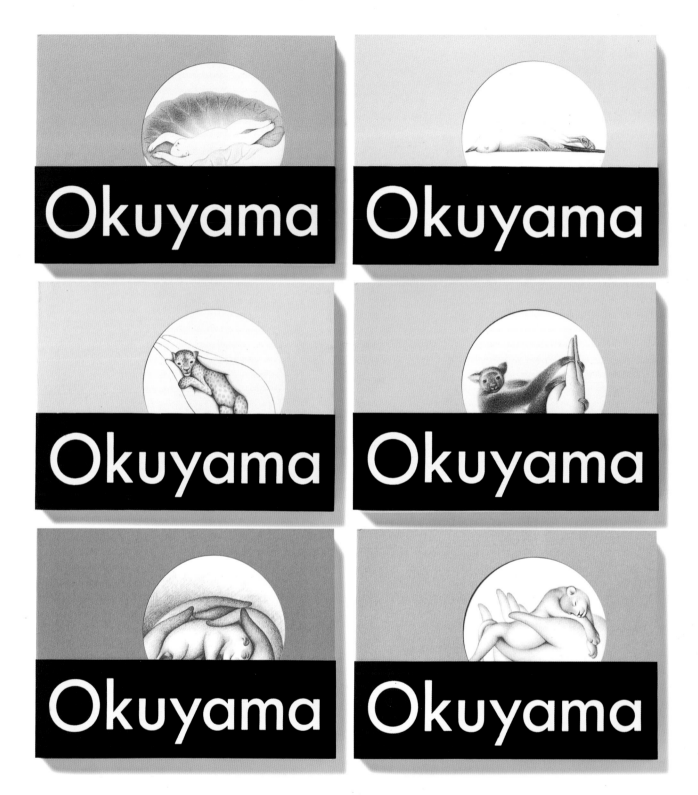

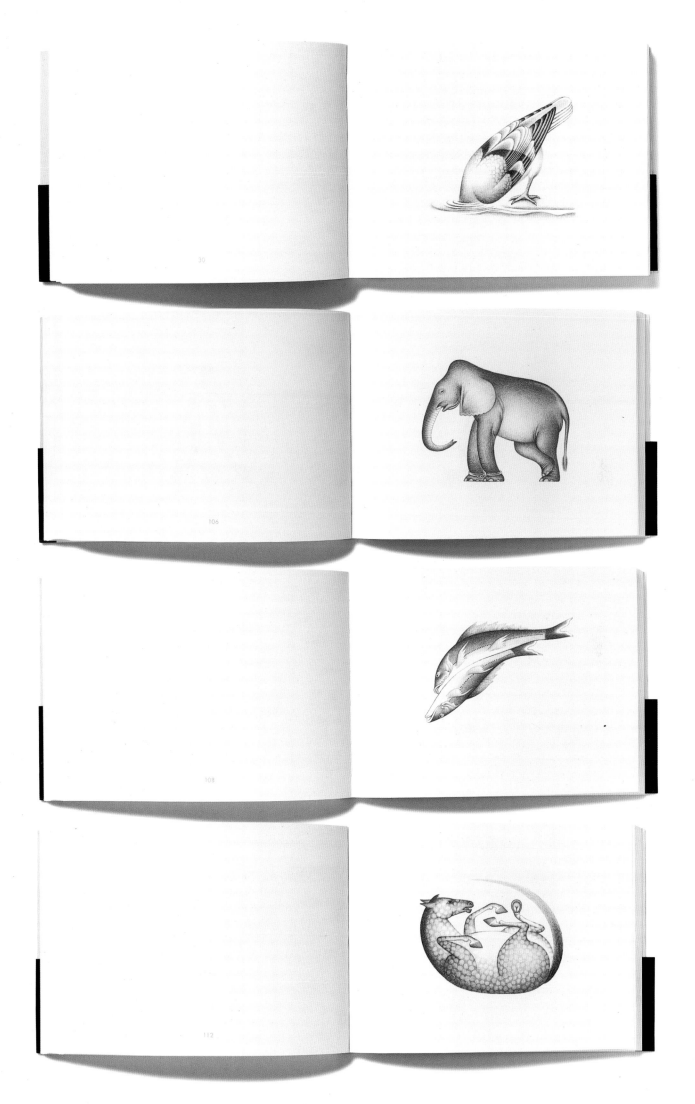

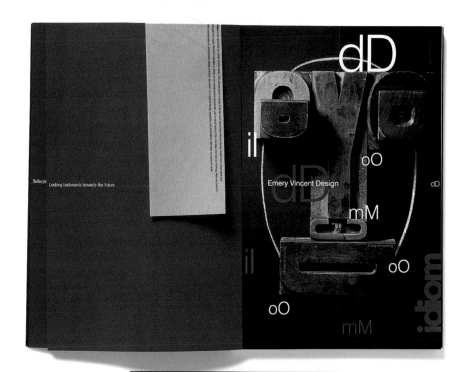

Design Firm, Client:
Emery Vincent Design
Creative Director,
Art Director:
Garry Emery
Designer: Emery Vincent
Design Team

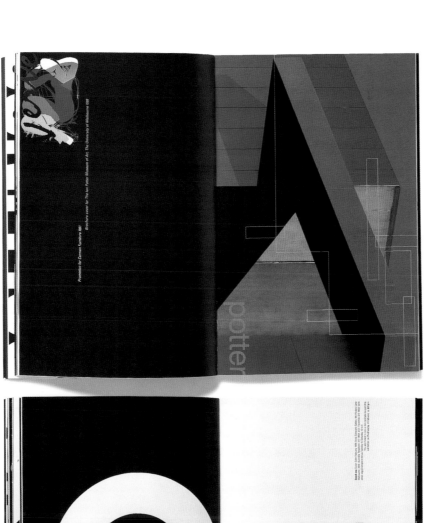

Promotion for Clement furniture 1997

Brochure cover for The late Potter Museum of Melbourne, The University of Melbourne 1999

Detail from Susan Cohn exhibition invitation 1999

Cohn me Susan Cohn February 16th Anna Schwartz Gallery 185 Flinders Lane Melbourne 3000 Australia Telephone 61 3 9654 6131 Facsimile 61 3 9650 3076 email magic@gaa.com.au Tuesday to Saturday 12 to 6

catch me

Gallery photography logotype 1992 Northern Territory Airport identity 1999

(this page)
Design Firm:
Hal Riney & Partners
Creative Director:
Vinny Chieco
Art Director:
Cynthia Murnane
Writer: Kammie
McArthur
Production Manager:
Jill Palmer
Photographer:
Dennis Murphy
Client:
Westmoor Farm

(opposite)
Design Firm:
Bianco & Cucco
Creative Directors,
Art Directors,
Designers:
Giovanni Bianco,
Susanna Cucco
Graphic Designer:
Simona Pavesi
Client: Gentry Portofino

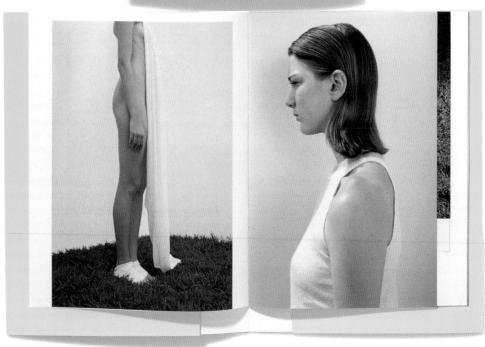

Design Firm: Bianco & Cucco
Creative Directors,
Art Directors:Giovanni Bianco,
Susanna Cucco
Photographer: Bettina Komenda
Client: Clone—Bruno Bordese

CLONE

Design Firm: Bianco & Cucco
Creative Directors,
Art Directors:Giovanni Bianco,
Susanna Cucco
Photographer: Bettina Komenda
Client: Clone—Bruno Bordese

(this and following spread)
Design Firm: Taku Satoh
Design Office
Creative Director, Art Director,
Designer: Taku Satoh
Photographer: Taishi Hirokawa
Client: Taku Satoh Design
Office Inc.

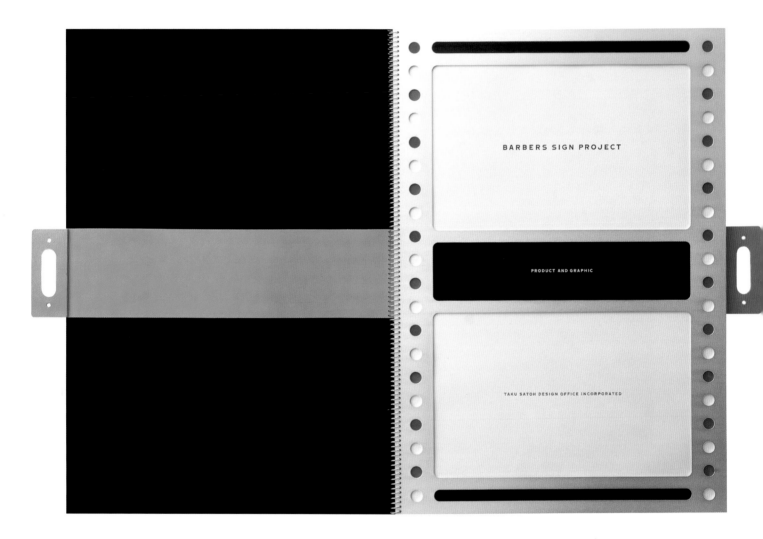

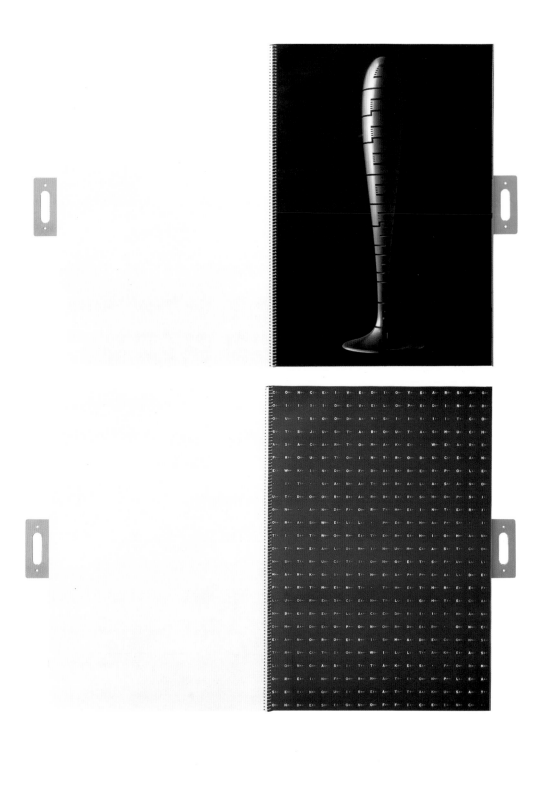

this is
tom

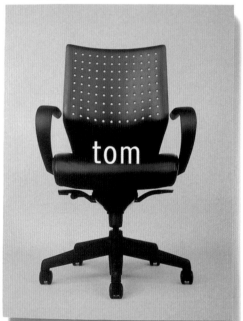

tom

Design Firm:
Concrete Design
Communications
Art Directors:
John Pylypczak,
Diti Katona
Designer, Writer:
John Pylypczak
Photographer:
Karen Levy
Client: Keilhauer
Industries

tom's   shy

tom is transfer red to Chicago

tom takes a   meeting

tom
can be bought

Please contact Keilhauer for your nearest representative
1 800 724 5665

(this page)
Design Firm:
Lahn Stafford Design
Art Director, Designer:
Dean Lahn
Writers: Dean Lahn,
Andrew Dunbar
Photographer:
Andrew Dunbar
Client: Wakefield Press

(opposite)
Design Firm: Instant
Corporate Culture
Creative Director:
Thomas Feicht
Art Director:
Manuela Nyhuis
Writers: Thomas Feicht,
Dr. Jean-Christophe

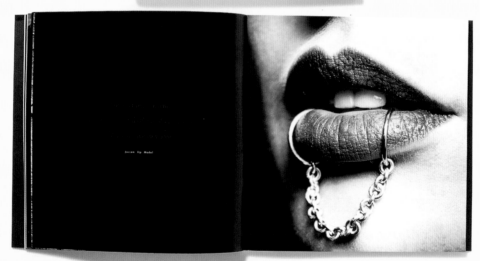

Ammann, Prof. Thomas
Bayrle, Michael
Schneider, Jan Teunen,
Tassilo von Grolman,
Peer Clahsen
Photographers:
Alexander Beck, Klaus
Weddig, Chris Kister,
Guido Deussen,
Alexander Geibel,
Michael Zirn, Angela
Görtsch, Ralf
Heidenreich, Patrick
Horcher, Leonid
Kamarowski, A.J.
Coordinators: Brigitte
Schecker, Annette
Mueller
Client: Maggi
Deutschland/Nestle

nur

DARE

Ellen J. Sussman, M.D.

*"The real challenge generated by the pressures of managed care is about value:
what does it cost, and what is the quality of the service? It's easy to raise quality – just raise costs.
And cutting costs is easy too. The really hard work is in increasing quality while reducing costs,
and this will provoke major change in the relationships among nurses, physicians, physician executives
and the community that uses the healthcare service. In the long run I believe this can be a
very beneficial process, but it's a change management problem of a very large scale.
The answers reside in the overall organization, not just with a single supervisor, or the CEO."*

President and CEO, Lehigh Valley Health Network

Charles Barnett

*"Instead of thinking strategic planning, we thought strategic themes, we thought about stakeholder
and community needs and connected them back to our mission and vision of the organization.
While this creates more uncertainty in the continuum from mission to deployable results,
it also creates more opportunities for flexibility. However, this approach is not a roadmap,
and therefore, the need for intense rigor in asking questions about choices is vital."*

President and CEO, Seton Health Network

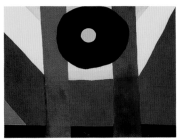

(this page)
Design Firm: Cook
& Shanosky Associates
Creative Director,
Art Director:
Roger Cook
Designers: Roger
Cook, Cathryn Cook,
Michael Milligan
Copywriter:
Katharine Watts
Client: Center for
Applied Research

(opposite)
Design Firm: Cahan
& Associates
Creative Director,
Art Director:
Bill Cahan
Designer: Sharrie Brooks
Photographers:
(pictured)
Lise Metzger,
Hugh Kretschmer
Client: Sharpe &
Associates

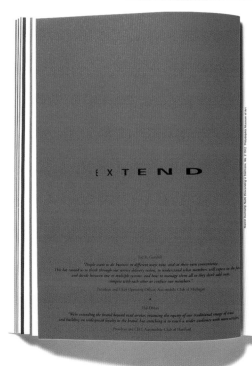

EXTEND

Jay R. Gambill

*"People want to do business in different ways now, and at their own convenience.
This has caused us to think through our service delivery vision, to understand what members will expect in the future
and decide between one or multiple systems, and how to manage them all so they don't add costs
nor compete with each other or confuse our members."*

President and Chief Operating Officer, Automobile Club of Michigan

Ed Deess

*"We're extending the brand beyond road service: retaining the equity of our traditional image of trust
and building on widespread loyalty to the brand, but stretching it to reach a wider audience with more services."*

President and CEO, Automobile Club of Hartford

lise metzger

hugh kretschmer

Design Firm: Design Guys
Creative Director,
Art Director,
Writer: Steven Sikora
Designer: Dawn Selg
Photographers: Lars Hansen,
Darrell Eager
Client: Target Stores

"At last we can afford to buy some
of the things we design."
—Michael Graves

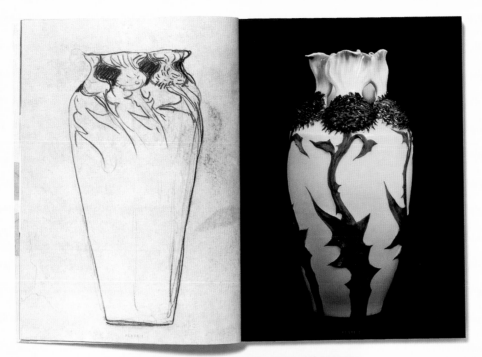

Design Firm:
Socio X
Creative Director,
Art Director:
Bridget de Socio
Designer:
Laura Harris
Photographer:
Noël Allum
Client:
Robert Schreiber

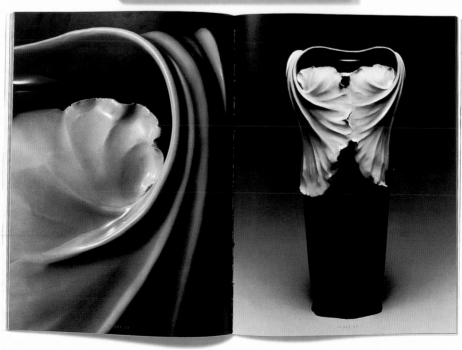

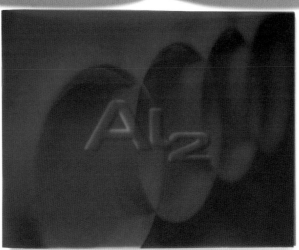

Design Firm: JVM
Werbeagentur GmbH
Creative Directors:
Mathias Jahn, Heiner Rogge
Art Director: Jörg Barre
Photographers: Iver Hansen,
Sigi Kercher
Client: Audi AG

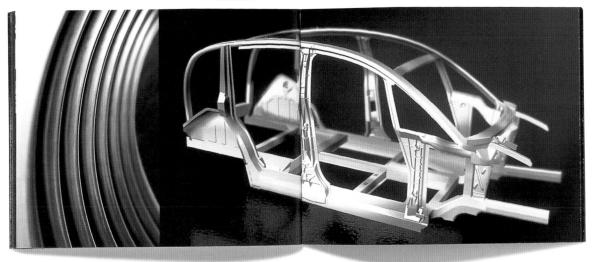

May 1999

CHROMA GRAPHICS, INC.

Sunday	Monday	Tuesday	Wednesday	Thursday	Friday	Saturday
						1
2	3	4	5	6	7	8
9	10	11	12	13	14	15
16	17	18	19	20	21	22
23 30	24 31	25	26	27	28	29

July 1999

CHROMA GRAPHICS, INC.

Sunday	Monday	Tuesday	Wednesday	Thursday	Friday	Saturday
				1	2	3
4	5	6	7	8	9	10
11	12	13	14	15	16	17
18	19	20	21	22	23	24
25	26	27	28	29	30	31

November 1999

CHROMA GRAPHICS, INC.

Sunday	Monday	Tuesday	Wednesday	Thursday	Friday	Saturday
	1	2	3	4	5	6
7	8	9	10	11	12	13
14	15	16	17	18	19	20
21	22	23	24	25	26	27
28	29	30				

December 1999

CHROMA GRAPHICS, INC.

Sunday	Monday	Tuesday	Wednesday	Thursday	Friday	Saturday
			1	2	3	4
5	6	7	8	9	10	11
12	13	14	15	16	17	18
19	20	21	22	23	24	25
26	27	28	29	30	31	

(opposite)
Design Firm: Johnson
Design Group
Creative Director: Len Johnson
Art Director: Norasack
Pathammavong
Designers: Daniel Conlan,
Norasack Pathammavong
Photographer: Bill Dempsey
Client: Chroma Graphics

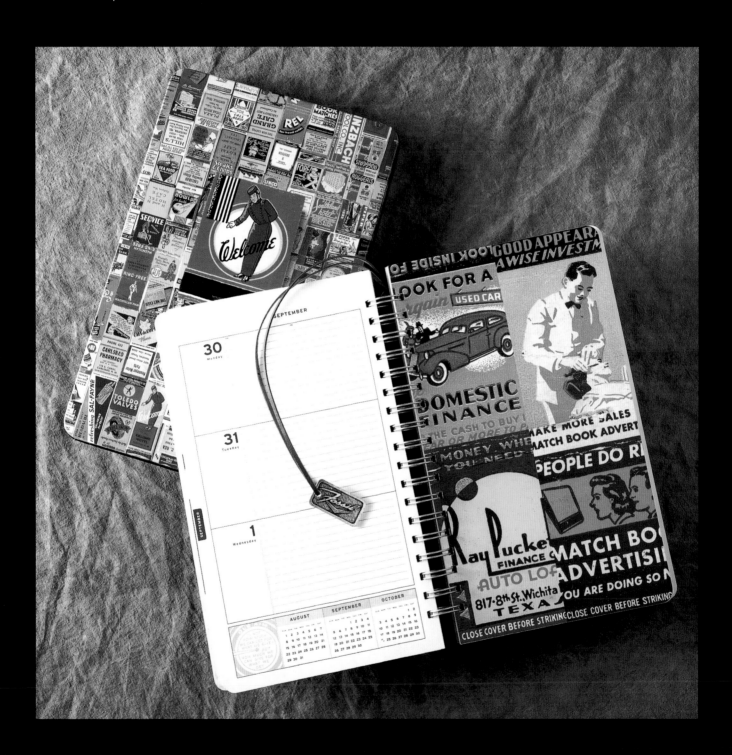

(this page)
Design Firm: Fossil
(in-house)
Creative Director,
Art Director: Tim Hale
Designers:
Casey McGarr,
Stephen Zhang,
John Dorcas, Jennifer Burk
Client: Fossil

1998

this is
not
tom's
agenda

Design Firm: Concrete
Design Communications
Art Directors: John
Pylypczak, Diti Katona
Designer: John Pylypczak
Photographer: Karen Levy
Client: Keilhauer Industries

january
1998

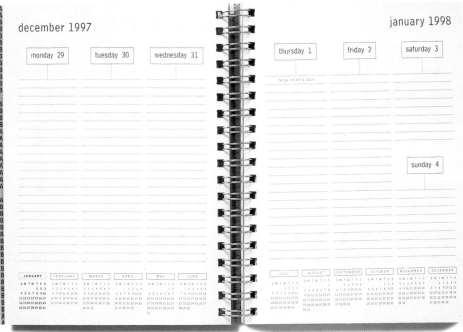

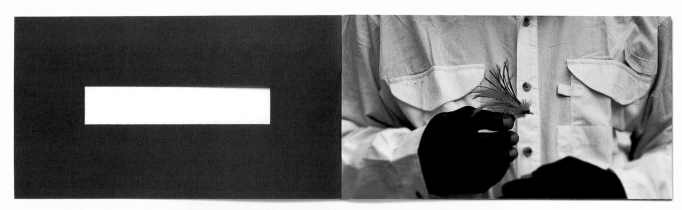

IM6 Trout Rods.

search

(opposite)
Design Firm: Riddell
Advertising & Design
Creative Director,
Writer: Jim Hagar
Art Director,
Designer:
Jeffrey Williamson
Photographers:
Terry Heffernan,
Andy Anderson
Calligrapher:
Georgia Deaver
Client: R.L. Winston
Rod Company

(this page)
Design Firm: Belk
Mignogna Associates
Creative Director:
Hans Neubert
Designers: Hans Neubert,
Jutta Kirchgeorg
Production:
Alberta Jarane
Client: Nonstøck

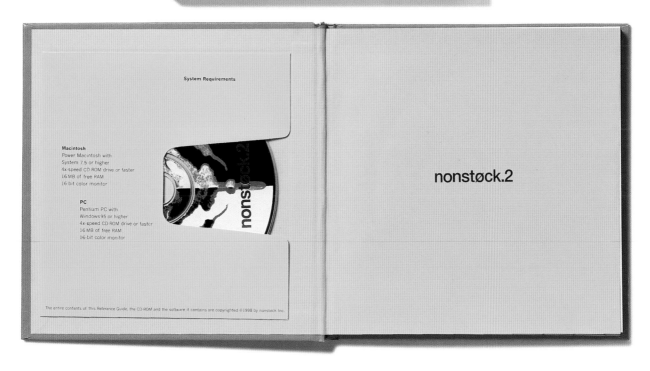

System Requirements

Macintosh
Power Macintosh with
System 7.5 or higher
4x-speed CD-ROM drive or faster
16 MB of free RAM
16-bit color monitor

PC
Pentium PC with
Windows 95 or higher
4x-speed CD-ROM drive or faster
16 MB of free RAM
16-bit color monitor

nonstøck.2

The entire contents of this Reference Guide, the CD-ROM and the software it contains are copyrighted ©1998 by nonstock Inc.

ESIG

S
AY
ES
RESOURCES
INOLOGIES
ION
SHOWS
AWARDS

ICO
TO
CO
NE
TE
FA
SL
ST

DESIGN EXHIBITION

Design Firm:
Büro X Design Gmbl
Creative Directors:
Andreas Miedaner,
Günter Eder
Art Director, Designe
Günter Eder
Graphic Designer:
Mario Buda
Client: Eichinger oder
Knechtl

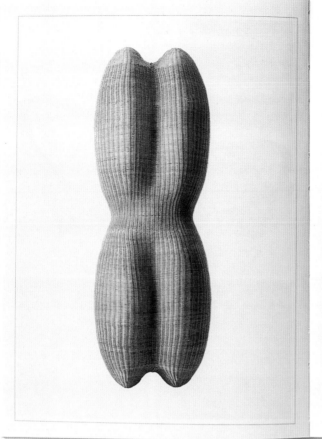

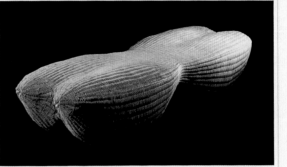

THIS LOUNGING DEVICE HAS A SIDE FOR DAY AND
A SIDE FOR NIGHT, LEANED AGAINST THE WALL,
THE OBJECT BECOMES IBU (MOTHER)

P: IBU
   WICKER LOUNGER
M: RATTAN

D: EOOS
   BERGMANN, BOHMANN, GRÜNDL - DESING
A: MARTIN BERGMANN
   HERNALSER HAUPTSTRASSE 17 / 31
   A - 1170 VIENNA
   TEL/FAX + 43 1 405 3987

TODAY

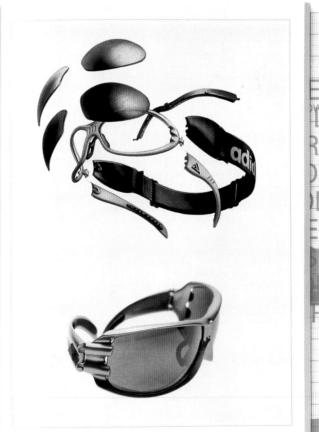

P: A 109 GALEFORCE
M: SPX
D: JOHANN SCHMIDTHALER

P: A 121 SPROCKET
M: SPX
P: A 252 STRIKER
M: SPX
D: GERHARD FUCHS

TODAY

Design Firm: Socio X
Creative Director: Deborah Moses
Art Director, Writer:
Bridget de Socio
Designer: Albert Lin
Photographer: Ruven Afonador
Client: Eagle's Eye

Choose your weapons. Cooking, like the art of war, requires the very finest. These exceptional knives can turn a dilettante into a master. The blades are handforged steel, the handles handcarved wood with horn, and the two are expertly crafted and perfectly balanced. TOP TO BOTTOM: Deba-bocho, for gutting and filleting fish, 7.12", [11A], $265. Nakiri-bocho, extra strong for chopping vegetables, 6.5", [11B], $125. Sushimi-bocho, for slicing fish, 8.75", [11D], $225. Usuba-bocho, for paring vegetables, 6", [11D], $175. Ajikiri-bocho, for filleting saurel, 3.75", [11E], $95. To maintain your knives, a whetstone is essential, [11F], $45.

Design Firm: Design: M/W
Creative Directors:
Allison Williams, J.P. Williams
Art Director:
Allison Williams
Designers: Allison Williams,
Mats Hakansson. Design
Assistant: Abigail Clawson
Photographer: Geof Kern,
Gentl & Hyers
Client: Takashimaya New York

Green is the original color. It represents new life, the earth's awakening, the thriving and flourishing natural landscape. From the luminous allure of emeralds to the familiar flash of a wad of fifties, it is various and everpresent. Green earthenware teapot, hand-thrown into an elegant, elongated shape by Japanese artist Uko Morita, 16 ozs., [1A], $125. Handcarved ebony tea scoop, [1B], $18. Super premium wild green tea–sencha–is harvested from the spot along the Yokimata river in Shizuoka, where it has been growing naturally for centuries. It has a refreshing bittersweet taste and light summer green color. Packaged in a natural bamboo container, 3.5 ozs., [1C], $38.

Vite, Dick se lave
les mains pour ne pas
faire attendre Jane.

Dick is very excited.
He washes his hands.
Twice.

Il y a de l'amour dans l'air

Love is in the air

Design Firm: Taxi
Advertising & Design
Creative Director:
Martin Beauvais
Designer:
Michael Lapointe
Writers: David Stortini
(English),
André Marois (French)
Photographer:
Andre Panneton
Client: Manager Jeans

Jane a gagné la partie en réussissant trois abats coup sur coup.
Quelle fille épatante!, pense Dick, admiratif.

Jane rolls three strikes in a row.
"What an amazing girl", Dick thinks admiringly.

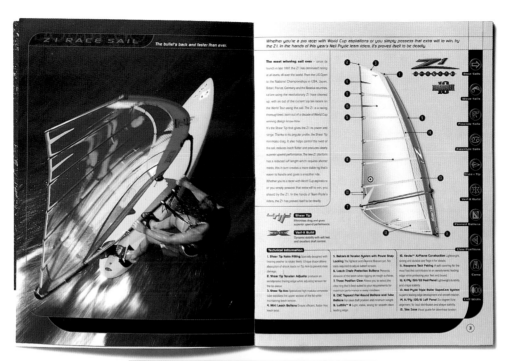

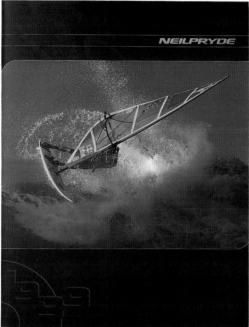

Design Firm:
Neil Pryde Marketing
Creative Director:
Simon Narramore
Art Director:
Gareth Walters
Designers: Grace Wong,
Wing Cheung
Writer: Chloe Lazar
Illustrator:
Wing Cheung
Web Design:
Frank Haasenritter
Photographers: Rick
Leeks (cover), Jono
Nicght, Eric Aeder,
Darrell Wong,
Gareth Brown, Simon
Narramore, Andrew
Chester Ong
Client: Neil Pryde Ltd.

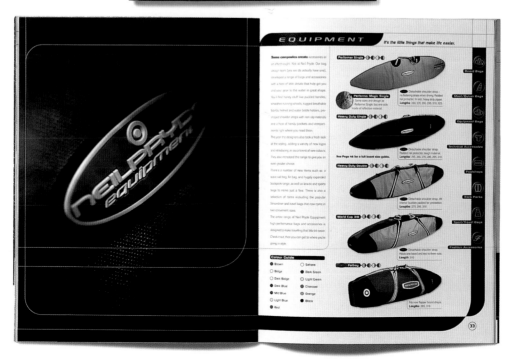

Design Firm: Sandstrom Design
Creative Director, Art Director,
Designer: Steve Sandstrom
Writer: Steve Sandoz. Client: Filmcore

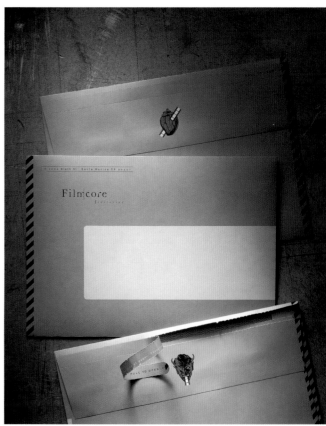

Design Firm: Pentagram Design
Partner/Designer:
Paula Scher
Designer: Anke Stohlmann
Client: Le Parker Meridien

Design Firm: Pentagram Design
Partner/Designer:
Paula Scher
Designer: Anke Stohlmann
Client: Le Parker Meridien

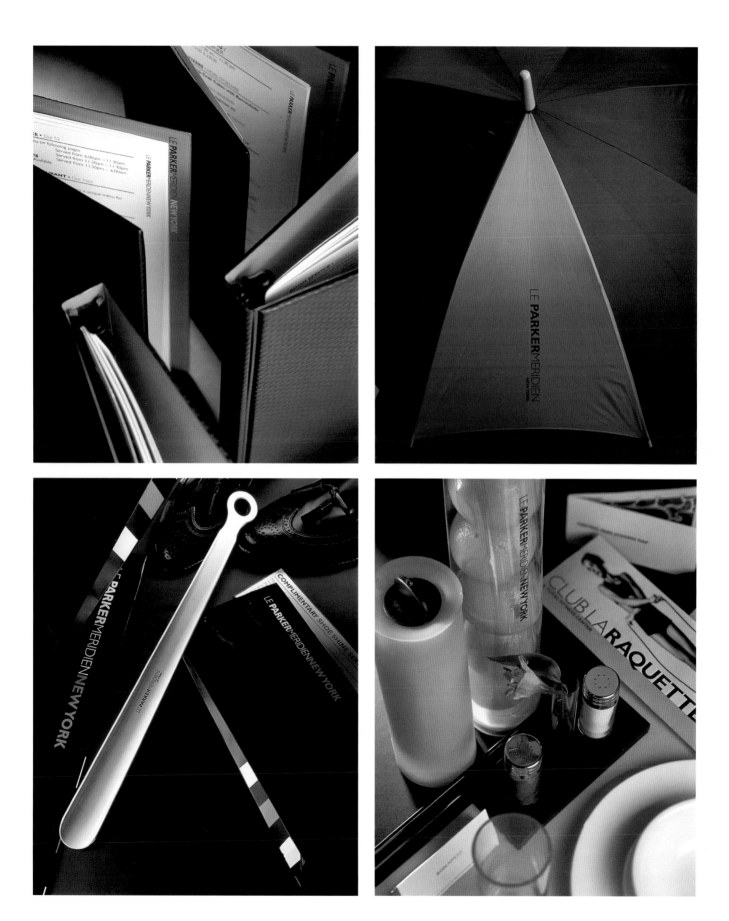

Design Firm:
Basler Design Group
Creative Director:
Bill Basler
Art Director:
Drew Davies
Designers: Bill Basler,
Drew Davies,
Bill Bollman
Client:
Basler Design Group

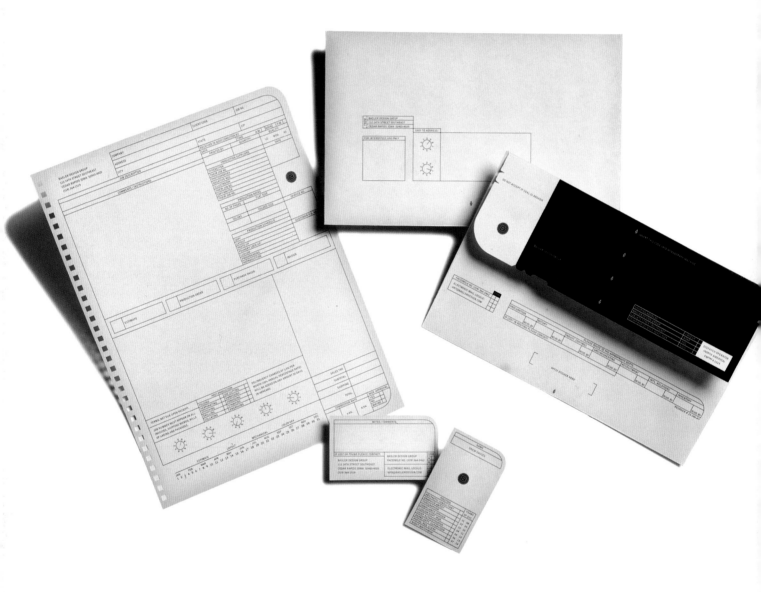

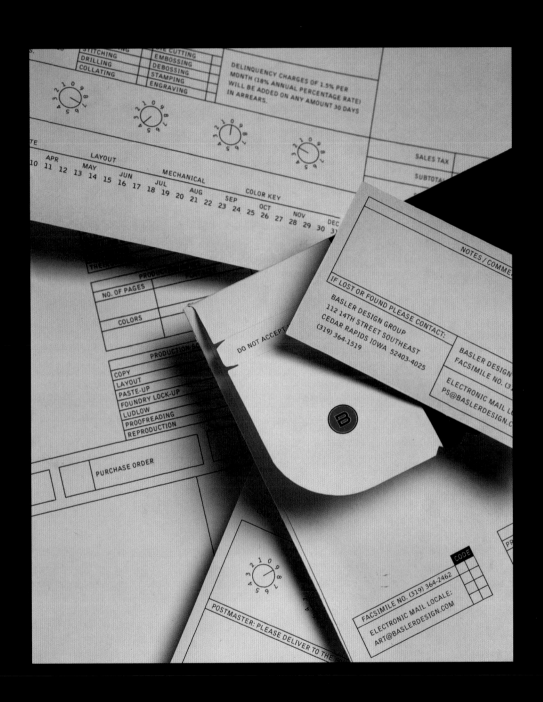

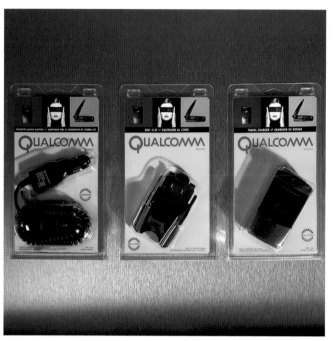

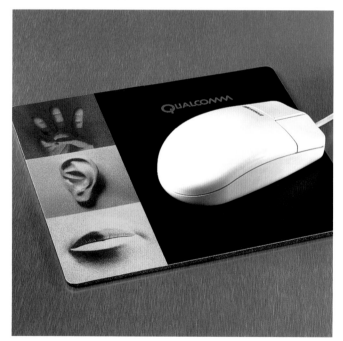
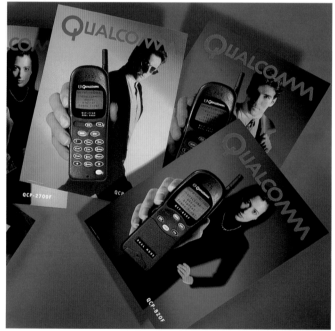

Design Firm: Mires Design
Creative Director, Art Director:
José A. Serrano
Designers: José A. Serrano,
Deborah Hom
Writer: Andrea May
Photographer: Carl Vanderschuit
Client: Qualcomm

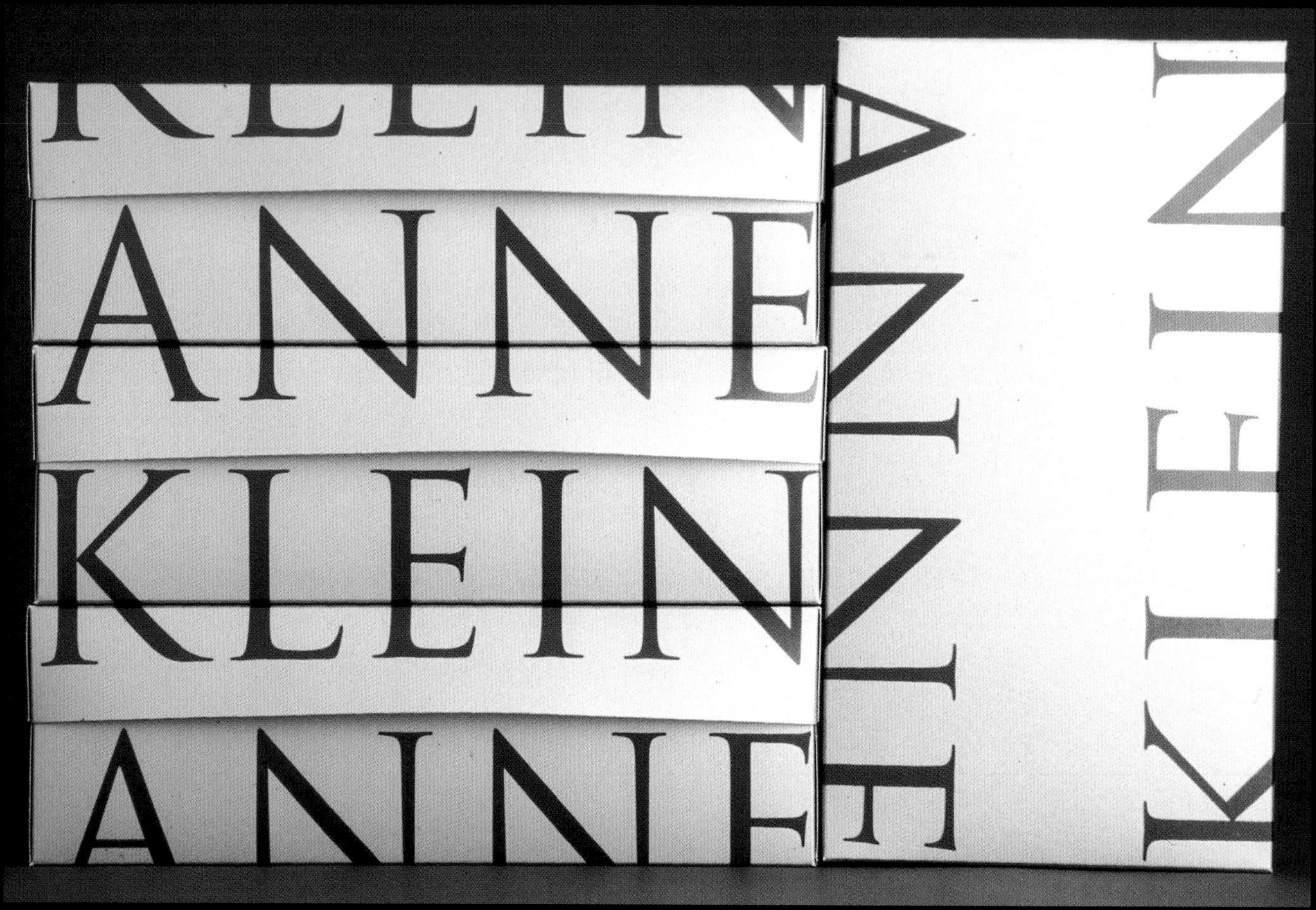
ANNE
KLEIN
ANNE
KLEIN

Design Firm:
Pentagram Design
Partner/Designer:
Paula Scher
Designer: Anke Stohlmann
Client: Anne Klein

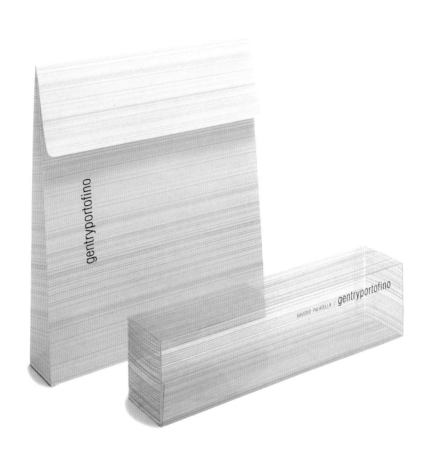

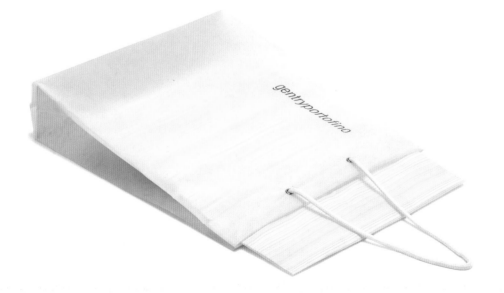

g

Gwyneth on a Roll No longer the ingenue, Gwyneth Paltrow has eased into stardom like Kate Hepburn into good gray flannels. With three movies set for release this season, she talks to Cathy Horyn about fame, her future and life after Brad. All clothes by Calvin Klein. Fashion editor: Sarajane Hoare Photographed by Patrick Demarchelier

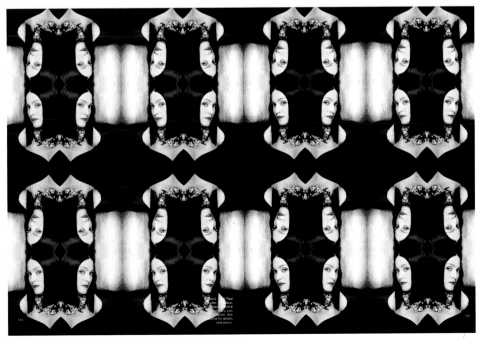

PAPER

CHRISTINA RICCI
SEX DOLL OR DEMON CHILD?
BY MICHAEL MUSTO

DON'T HATE ME BECAUSE I'M A CONTROL FREAK
BY KIM HASTREITER

SUBVERSIVE CINEASTE TODD SOLONDZ

UNKLE MUSIC'S NEXT BIG THING?

GOTH STYLE EVERY DAY IS HALLOWEEN

PAPER

IT'S MILLA TIME!
THE RIPENING OF MILLA JOVOVICH

PARIS FASHION

SKATE PORN

DAFT PUNK, FOLK IMPLOSION

JUSTIN PIERCE

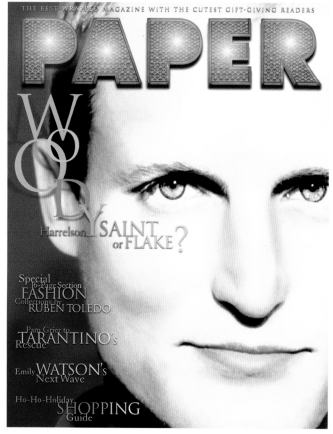

PAPER

WOODY
Harrelson SAINT or FLAKE?

Special 16-Page Section
FASHION
Collections by RUBEN TOLEDO

Pam Grier to TARANTINO's Rescue

Emily WATSON's Next Wave

Ho-Ho-Holiday
SHOPPING Guide

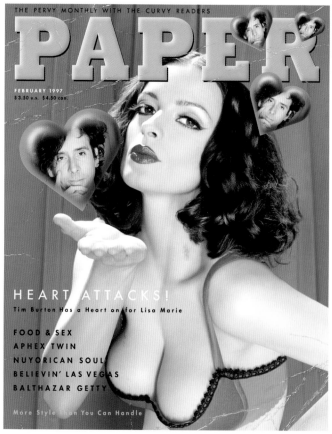

PAPER

FEBRUARY 1997
$3.50 u.s. $4.50 can.

HEART ATTACKS!
Tim Burton Has a Heart on for Lisa Marie

FOOD & SEX
APHEX TWIN
NUYORICAN SOUL
BELIEVIN' LAS VEGAS
BALTHAZAR GETTY

More Style Than You Can Handle

(opposite, top left)
Design Firm: Socio X
Creative Director: Bridget de Socio
Designer: Jason Endres
Photographer: Robert Fleischauer
Client: *Paper* Magazine

(opposite, top right)
Design Firm: Socio X
Creative Director: Bridget de Socio
Designer: Ninja V. Oertzen
Photographer: Albert Sanchez
Client: *Paper* Magazine

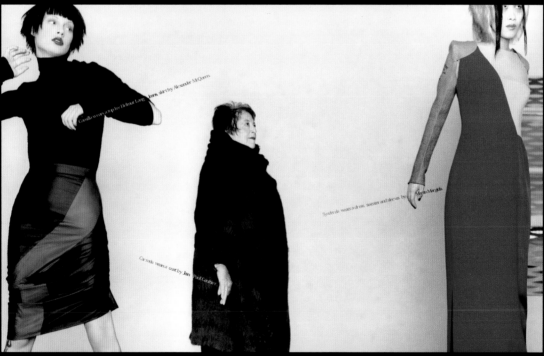

(opposite, bottom left)
Design Firm: Socio X
Creative Director:
Bridget de Socio
Designer: Ninja V. Oertzen
Client: *Paper* Magazine

(opposite, bottom right)
Design Firm: Socio X
Creative Director: Bridget de Socio
Designer: Ninja V. Oertzen
Photographer: Dah Len
Client: *Paper* Magazine

(previous spread, right page)
Design Firm: Socio X
Creative Director: Bridget de Socio
Designer: Ninja V. Oertzen
Photographer: Norma Zuniga
Client: *Paper* Magazine

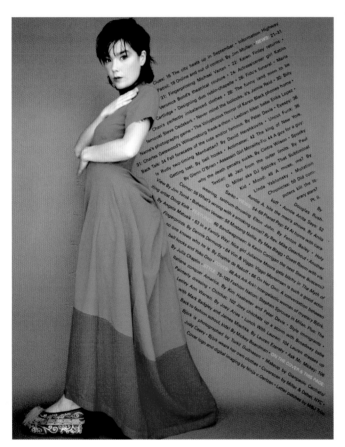

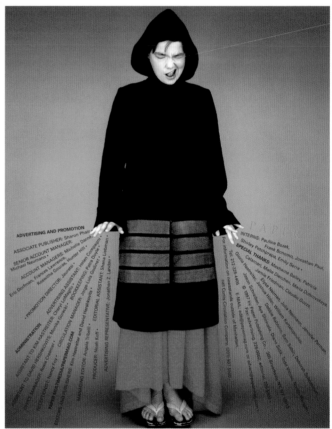

(this page)
Design Firm: Socio X
Creative Director: Bridget de Socio
Designer: Ninja V. Oertzen
Photographer: Torkil Gudnason
Client: *Paper* Magazine

(opposite)
Design Firm: Socio X
Creative Director: Bridget de Socio
Designer: Ninja V. Oertzen
Photographer: Michael Williams
Client: *Paper* Magazine

head wrap by Rifat Ozbek, shoes by Sonoky, earrings from Patricia Field

SCRATCH
'n' style

Come in, selector. In 1968, the granddaddy of dub reggae, Lee "Scratch" Perry—producer/innovator/eccentric extraordinaire and one of the most influential players in reggae history—formed the Upsetter record label to provide a platform for the talent in Kingston, Jamaica. Among the original acts on Upsetter were the legendary Wailers— Bunny Livingston, Peter Tosh and Bob Marley—and King Tubby. Perry is perhaps best known for his pioneering dub techniques— a studio sound characterized by track muting and reverb effects. Hip-hop, trip-hop and jungle all have their roots in this style. Today, dubmaster Perry is as fresh as ever.

A recent collaboration with the U.K.'s Mad Professor produced some wicked mixes of dub and jungle tracks.

We present a tribute to back-home/backyard style and fashion. To the original Upsetter, give thanks, + Tess Daly

Photographs by Michael Williams/Jelly Casey

Styling and realization by Carmel Niamo/Jelly Carey

Special thanks to Maria C. Yhayoma

dress by Sonoky, shoes by Miu Miu, socks by Birkenstock, bag by Fendi

(this page)
Design Firm: Gusev Design
Creative Director, Writer: Yuri Katsman
Art Director, Designer: Anatoly Gusev
Illustrator: Andrei Biljo, Leonid Firsov
Photographer: Rez Van
Client: *Dengi* (Money) Magazine

(opposite)
Design Firm:
American Way Magazine (in-house)
Art Director: Scott Feaster
Designer: Charles Stone
Photographer: Allen Kapahi / Susan
Cummins Gallery
Client: American Airlines

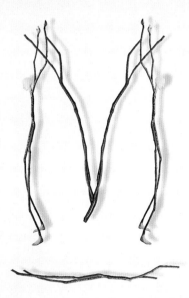

M A R G A R E T   F O R D

BRECHT 100

XXXI. ÉVF. 11. SZÁM 1998. NOVEMBER

WILS

RON

ARREDAMENTO

TASARIM
KÜLTÜRÜ
DERGİSİ

1998/11 450 000 TL

MİMARLIK

PROFİL:
DANIEL
LIBESKIND

DOSYA:
YAZI VE MİMARLIK

ARREDAMENTO

TASARIM
KÜLTÜRÜ
DERGİSİ

1998/07-08 450 000 TL

MİMARLIK

PROFİL:
ARQUITECTONICA

DOSYA:
MİMARLIK
VE POLİTİKA

SÖYLEŞİ

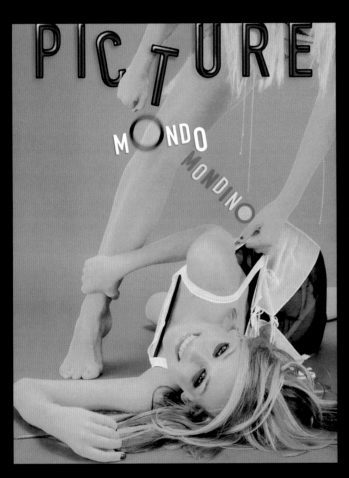

(this page, left)
Design Firm: Socio X
Creative Director, Art Director,
Writer: Bridget de Socio
Designer: Albert Lin, Lara Harris
Photographer:
Jean Bapiste Mondino

30TH ANNIVERSARY SPECIAL

Rolling Stone

WE'RE OFF...
Seinfeld Hits the Road!

Rolling Stone

Life After Death Row

SNOOP DOGGY DOGG IS BACK!

SWING REVIVAL

Is It Jumpin' Or Just Jive?

Blood, Dust And Tears

INSIDE MEXICO'S SECRET WAR

The Original
HOT List

STARRING
This Year's Model
Laetitia
Casta

Rolling Stone

Slay Lady Slay
SARAH MICHELLE GELLAR
AND THE POWER OF
BUFFY-HOOD

SPRING BREAK '98
THE ESSENTIAL GUIDE TO THE TOP PARTY DESTINATIONS

P.J. O'ROURKE IN ALBANIA

POT BARS IN VANCOUVER

PEARL JAM LIVE IN MAUI

MADONNA HER BEST ALBUM IN A DECADE

ROBBIE ROBERTSON AN AMERICAN JOURNEY

GRATEFUL DEAD TO TOUR?

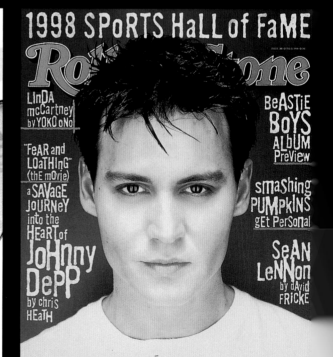

1998 SPORTS HALL of FAME

Rolling Stone

LINDA McCARTNEY by YOKO ONO

"FEAR and LOATHING" (THE MOVIE) a SAVAGE JOURNEY into the HEART of JOHNNY DEPP by CHRIS HEATH

BEASTIE BOYS ALBUM PREVIEW

SMASHING PUMPKINS GET PERSONAL

SEAN LENNON by DAVID FRICKE

(opposite)
Design Firm: *Rolling Stone* (in-house)
Art Director, Designer:
Fred Woodward
Photographers: Mark Seliger
(Cast of Seinfeld, Sarah Michelle
Gellar); Herb Ritts (Laetitia Casta); Dan
Winters (Johnny Depp)
Photo Editor: Rachel Knepfer
Client: *Rolling Stone*

(this page)
Design Firm: *Rolling Stone* (in-house)
Art Director: Fred Woodward
Designers: Fred Woodward,
Gail Anderson
Photographer: Mark Seliger
Photo Editor: Rachel Knepfer
Client: *Rolling Stone*

AFTER BEING TOLD HER ALBUM WAS A FLOP AND HER TOUR WAS A BUST, SHE DID WHAT SHE KNOWS BEST—SHE WORKED HARDER. A YEAR IN THE LIFE OF JANET

BY DAVID RITZ

SEX, SADNESS & THE TRIUMPH OF JANET JACKSON

THE MYSTERY is the low flame that burns around the perimeters of Janet Jackson's soul. The flame feeds off the most highly combustible elements: survival and ambition, caution and creativity, supreme confidence and dark fear. The flame is a sensual thing. The power and purity of deep sexuality surely fuel the flame. Even when Janet doesn't speak – even when, as is often her habit, she silences silences to speak for her – you sense something burning within. A secret, a poem, a song. FOR YEARS, she has burned with the need to say what she has not been able to say before: that

Opposite page: Janet, with Rexd. Despite Hair differences, they are two halves of a whole, a study in yin-yang.

PHOTOGRAPH BY MARK SELIGER

(this page, top and opposite, top)
Design Firm: *Rolling Stone* (in-house)
Art Director: Fred Woodward
Designers: Fred Woodward,
Hannah McCaughey
Typographer: Hannah McCaughey
Photographer: Mark Seliger
Photo Editor: Rachel Knepfer
Client: *Rolling Stone*

(this page, bottom)
Design Firm: *Rolling Stone* (in-house)
Art Director: Fred Woodward
Designers: Fred Woodward,
Gail Anderson
Typographer: Eric Siry
Photographer: Mark Seliger
Photo Editor: Rachel Knepfer
Client: *Rolling Stone*

HIS JOURNEY

FROM NERDY NEW YORK KID
TO HIP HOLLYWOOD ROYALTY PROVES

THERE'S SOMETHING ABOUT BEN STILLER

by Chris Mundy

BEN STILLER'S LOS ANGELES apartment is striking for a number of reasons (the penthouse deck with a view of the Wilshire Country Club springs to mind), but what stands out most is why he feels at home there. "What I really like," says Stiller as he shows you around, "is that it feels like a New York apartment."

He's right. Much like Stiller himself, the home seems slightly out of place in the high glare of Hollywood, more subdued, the kind of space as likely to have the curtains drawn as it is to have the sun pouring in.

Stiller points out the hardwood floors, the Twenties-style kitchen, the original moldings. In the large main room of the duplex's bottom floor, there is a collection of black-and-white photographs, nothing else – like a SoHo gallery space.

As he gives the tour, Stiller is warm; yet, for someone who has made his mark in comedy, he does not strike you as the casual sort. He is unfailingly polite; he is friendly; but there is also a quiet intensity and a nervousness that seeps into the air around him. You like him. You just wouldn't call him to entertain at a child's birthday party.

"I've never really felt like a funny, funny guy," says Stiller as we make our way to the deck. "I've never really felt like Mr. Life of the Party. People who know me know that I'm not the most gregarious person. I'm trying to open myself up more. I've realized in the last few years that my state of mind affects how I live my life."

Stiller's mind these days must be in a dizzy state – a career high induced by the sheer goofiness and phenomenal success of *There's Something About Mary*. Stiller has always been one of the most versatile talents of his generation: an Emmy-winning writer (for *The Ben Stiller Show*); a director of major stars in major motion pictures (Winona Ryder in *Reality Bites*, Jim Carrey in *The Cable Guy*); and a steadily em-

ployed actor drawn to small, intriguing comedies such as *Flirting With Disaster, Zero Effect* and the controversial *Your Friends and Neighbors*. But rarely have the heavens been better aligned for a performer than they are now for Stiller. First comes *There's Something About Mary*, the summer comedy that won't quit even deep into the fall and the kind of colossal hit that every star needs. At the same time, Stiller nails a performance as a junkie TV writer in *Permanent Midnight* that most serious actors saw was a lifetime to deliver. After a career spent working diligently, Stiller has finally hit

their parents out of town, the two would fill the void with show business. Not surprisingly, both are now actors. From the moment Ben began to look at the world around him, he has been building his body of work.

"Ben and Amy did a lot of films together," says Anne Meara. "They would do show tunes and do our act. We weren't there a lot, and I think that was painful for them."

"But we didn't want to go to L.A.," says Jerry. "We thought a bigger danger was growing up in a community where the neighbors were all stars and the kids were in competition with their parents' roles."

The irony is that while his parents agonized over whether to live in New York or Los Angeles, Stiller was learning texts at the entertainment industry. Today, at thirty-two, Stiller lives comfortably in all three.

SCENE 2 : AS STILLER lounges on his deck in L.A., he taps back in his chair and tries to make some sense of it all. He has spent a great deal of time in therapy – "I haven't been going for about a year, but I actually really like it," he says – and his approach to answers often seems rooted in these sessions.

"I'm working on that whole happiness-balance issue in life," says Stiller. "I think you're always working on that. I tend to lean more toward the work side of life. It's important to find happiness outside of your work."

Yet, if you listen to the people who know him best, you wonder how precarious that balance really is.

His friend (and *Permanent Midnight* momeister) Jerry Stahl: "I've never seen anybody put in the three man-

hours Ben does. Being a forty-five-year-old guy with a liver that lives in an adjoining county, I sure as hell can't keep up. It's amazing."

His father: "He works much too hard, for my money. I just wish he would take a rest."

His friend and frequent collaborator Janeane Garofalo: "He works harder than anyone I know. He never, ever, ever is not working. It's actually bizarre."

Not that Stiller seems unhappy. On the contrary, as he sits on his deck, feet propped up, Stiller is content, almost unable to imagine another way of life. It's as if because

him found them on Eighty-fourth Street in Manhattan.

Stiller's apartment was on Riverside Drive; his best friend lived on Central Park West; in between was Brandale High School. "Those four or five blocks were like a gauntlet," remembers Stiller. "I used to live in fear of these Brandale kids."

"One day he was mugged twice, once on the East Side and once on the West Side," says Jerry Stiller. He laughs. "And once they came back and said, 'We don't like this watch.'"

All this helped young Ben evolve a personal style of film. "One guy would get mugged and then we'd run after them through Riverside Park," recalls Stiller of his earliest works. "They all had names like *They Called It Murder* or *Murder in the Park.*"

As Stiller's adult career blossomed, it followed a similar path – *The Ben Stiller Show* showcased his ability to ape his favorite movies before honing in on his darker depths. Yet Stiller's range almost never came to light. Perhaps having missed his dramatic turn in *They Called It Murder*, the producers of *Permanent Midnight* first offered Stiller's role to David Duchovny and too, this is not a typo) Jon Bon Jovi. Even Stiller had his doubts.

"The biggest challenge was convincing myself that I was allowed to play that part," Stiller says. "I was fascinated by it. There were a lot of similarities as far as Jerry Stahl as a person – this Jewish comedy writer in L.A."

Based on Stahl's autobiography of his descent into the hells of heroin and Hollywood, the film is as relentless at any in recent memory, and Stiller – who barely ate during the course of filming – is riveting.

"Meeting Jerry and talking about this role really changed me as a person," says Stiller. "The key for me was that he showed me I didn't have to be a drug addict to understand why addicts take drugs – it's about not wanting to feel pain. I figured out what I did in my

---

The End

BY CHRIS HEATH

The 180th and final episode of "Seinfeld," to be broadcast on May 14th, was scheduled to be filmed over nine days, from March 31st to April 8th. ROLLING STONE was there the whole time – for more than 100 hours on set – watching. Hiding in corners. Being nosy. All Jerry Seinfeld asked in return was that the ensuing story not reveal anything. This is that story.

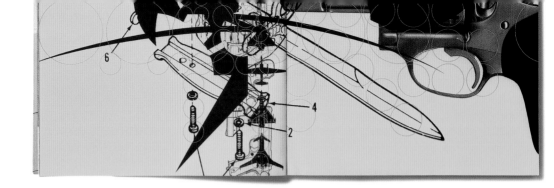

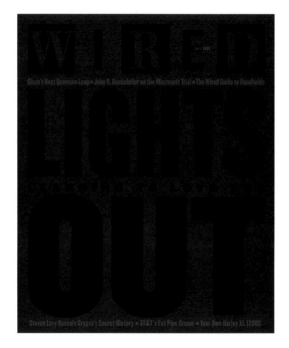

WIRED

Cisco's Next Quantum Leap • John D. Rockefeller on the Microsoft Trial • The Wired Guide to Handhelds

LIGHTS

OUT

Steven Levy Reveals Crypto's Secret History • AT&T's Fat Pipe Dream • Tour Our Harley XL 1200S

(opposite, bottom)
Design Firm: Punkt
Creative Director: Thomas Schneider
Art Director, Designer,
Photographer: Giles Dunn
Writer: Matt Groening
Client: *Wired* Magazine

(opposite, top)
Design Firm: Punkt
Creative Director: John Plunkett

Art Director, Designer:
Giles B. Dunn
Writer: Amy Jo Kim
Photographer: Giles B. Dunn,
Photonica
Client: *Wired* Magazine

(opposite, middle)
Design Firm: *Wired* Magazine
Designer Director:
Thomas Schneider

(this page, left)
Design Firm: Exquisite Corporation
Creative Directors:
Riley John-Donnell,
Richard Klein
Art Director, Designer:
Riley John-Donnell
Client: *Surface* Magazine

(this page, right)
Design Firm: Exquisite Corporation
Creative Directors: Riley
John-Donnell, Richard Klein
Art Director, Designer:
Riley John-Donnell
Photographer: Thomas Schenk
Client: *Surface* Magazine

STORIA DI COPERTINA PATRICIA ARQUETTE E LE ATTRICI SIMBOLO
DI UNA NUOVA FEMMINILITÀ PREGIUDIZI PERCHÉ LE DONNE SONO LE
PEGGIORI NEMICHE DELLE DONNE NUCLEARE 12 ANNI DOPO
CHERNOBYL L'ITALIA È ANCORA RADIOATTIVA? IN VIAGGIO SUGGESTIONI
FIAMMINGHE TRA LE CASE MERLATE DI BRUGES MISTERI RUSSI SPIE
PER AMORE E PER DENARO ALL'OMBRA DEL KGB

IL FEMMINILE DEL CORRIERE DELLA SERA

(this page)
Design Firm:
Cento Per Cento SRL
Art Director,
Designer:
Pier Paolo Pitacco
Photographer:
Gerry Avemaim
Client: Rizzoli,
Io Donna Magazine

(opposite)
Design Firm:
Frost Design Ltd
Art Director:
Vince Frost
Designers: Vince Frost,
Derek Samuel,
Elaine Perks
Client: D & AD

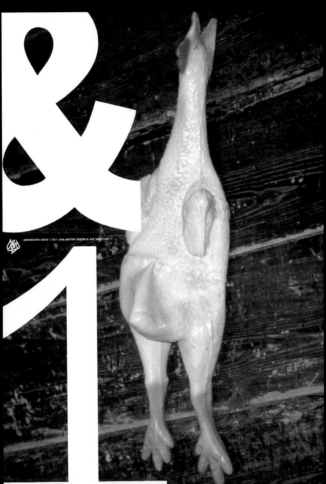

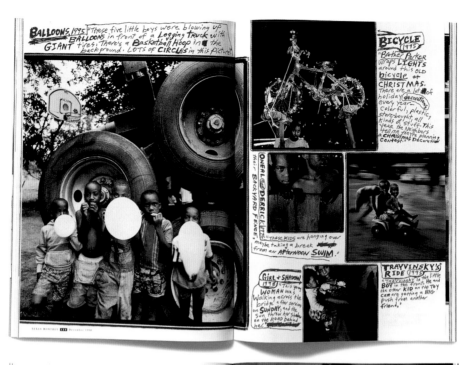

(this page, top and bottom)
Design Firm:
Texas Monthly
(in-house)
Creative Director,
Art Director:
D.J. Stout
Designers:
D.J. Stout,
Nancy McMillen
Writer:
Anne Dingus
Photographer:
O. Rufus Lovett
Client:
Texas Monthly

(this page, middle)
Design Firm:
Texas Monthly
(in-house)
Creative Director,
Art Director:
D.J. Stout
Designers:
D.J. Stout,
Nancy McMillen
Writer:
Skip Hollandsworth
Photographer:
Don Glentzer
Client:
Texas Monthly

(opposite)
Design Firm:
Tove L. Nilsen
Art Director,
Designer:
Tove Nilsen
Client: Tique AS

life's a **b each!**

Enten du vil eller ikke - bikinisesongen er her. Vi kan ikke hjelpe deg med uønskede valker (bortsett fra å si at du er fin som du er, uansett!), men vi kan vise deg noen av bikini-modellene som vil dukke opp på stranden i sommer.
Foto: Magda

Bikini fra Ralph Lauren, kr 1100.

MIRAKEL? MINUS 10 ÅR PÅ 10 DAGER!

TIQUE

design

HJEMME HOS MOTEMOGULEN
HYBRIDKUNSTNERNE • DET VONDE I OSS
GIPSY ROSE • MOTE MØTER MAT
HÅRFIN HØST • ROCKA POPDAMER
MAXIMALISMENS HEVN

Nr. 7 1998 - kr 45,-

kick off!

Vi sparker igang vårt jubileumsår med designere som har

inspirert og gledet oss gjennom 15 år. Foto: Bjørn Opsahl

(opposite)
Design Firm: Swieter Design US
Creative Director: Mark Ford
Art Director: John Swieter
Designer: Cameron Smith
Client: DART
(Dallas Area Rapid Transit)

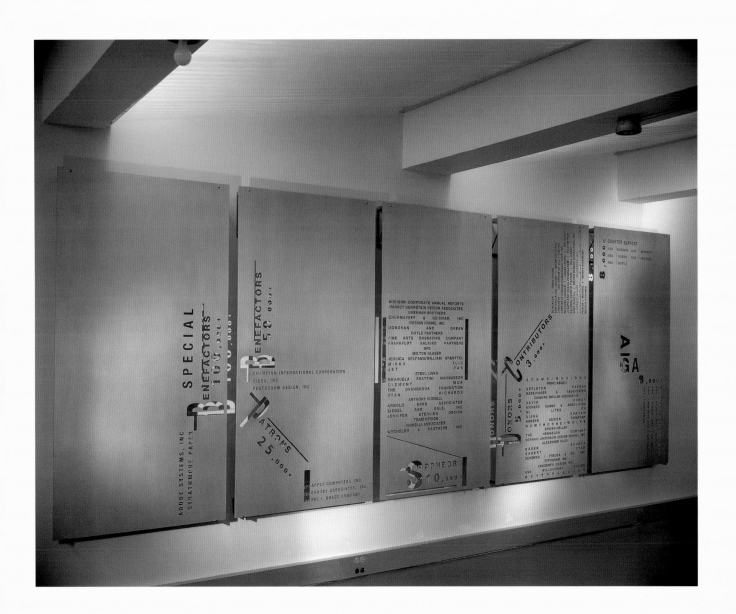

(this page)
Design Firm:
Jennifer Sterling Design
Creative Director,
Art Director,
Designer, Illustrator:
Jennifer Sterling
Client: AIGA

Partner/Architect:
James Biber
Associate/Architect:
Michael Zweck-Brommer
Partner/Graphic Designer:
Michael Bierut
Graphic Designer:
Esther Bridavsky
Photographer: James Shanks
Client: Fashion Center

Design Firm: Lorenc Design
Art Director: Jan Lorenc
Designer: Chung Youl Yoo
Architect: Steve McCall
Interior Designer: Janice McCall
Photographer: Rion Rizzo /
Creative Sources Photography
Client: Donut King

(this spread)
Design Firm: Duffy Design
and Interactive
Creative Director: Joe Duffy
Art Director: Kobe
Designers: Kobe, Jason Strong,
Dan Olson
Writer: Marty Senn, Lisa Pemerick
Photographer: Dana Wheelock
Client: Retail Concepts

(following spread)
Design Firm: Pentagram Design
Partner/Architect: James Biber
Associate/Architect Michael
Zweck-Bronner
Architect: Jim Cleary
Partner/Designer: Michael Gericke
Designers: Su Mathews, Maggie West
Photographer: Andrew Bordwin
Client: UPS World Services Store

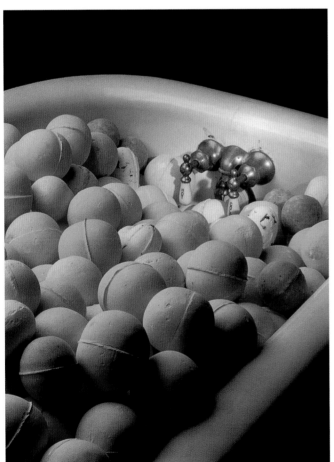

(this and following spread)
Design Firm: Lorenc Design
Creative Director,
Art Director: Jan Lorenc
Designer: John Lauer
Graphic Designer: Rory Myers
Architect: Gary Flesher
Photographer: Rion Rizzo /
Creative Sources Photography
Client: Georgia Pacific

(this and following spread)
Design Firm: Lorenc Design
Creative Director,
Art Director: Jan Lorenc
Designer: John Lauer
Graphic Designer: Rory Myers
Architect: Gary Flesher
Photographer: Rion Rizzo /
Creative Sources Photography
Client: Georgia Pacific

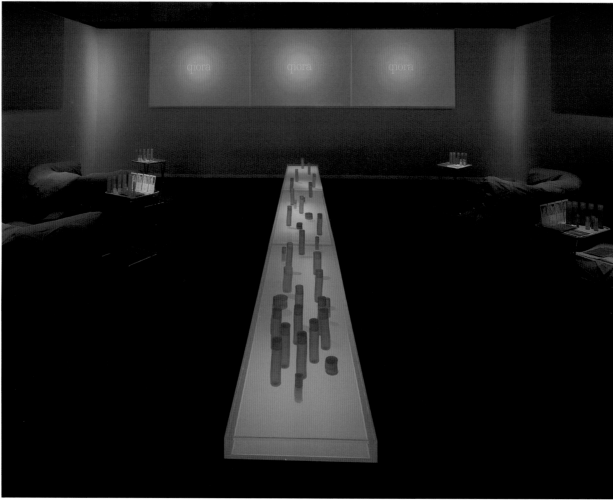

Design Firm: Shiseido Creation DVS
Creative Director: Shyuichi Ikeda
Art Director: Aoshi Kudo
Designers: Aoshi Kudo, Rikiya Vekusa
Film Director: Hiroyuki Nakano
Lighting Designer: Harumi Fujimoto
Client: Shiseido Co., Ltd.

Design Firm: Shiseido Creation DVS
Creative Director: Shyuichi Ikeda
Art Director: Aoshi Kudo
Designers: Aoshi Kudo, Rikiya Vekusa
Film Director: Hiroyuki Nakano
Lighting Designer: Harumi Fujimoto
Client: Shiseido Co., Ltd.

Design Firm: Shiseido Creation DVS
Creative Director: Masao Ohta
Art Director, Designer: Aoshi Kudo
Client: Shiseido Co., Ltd.

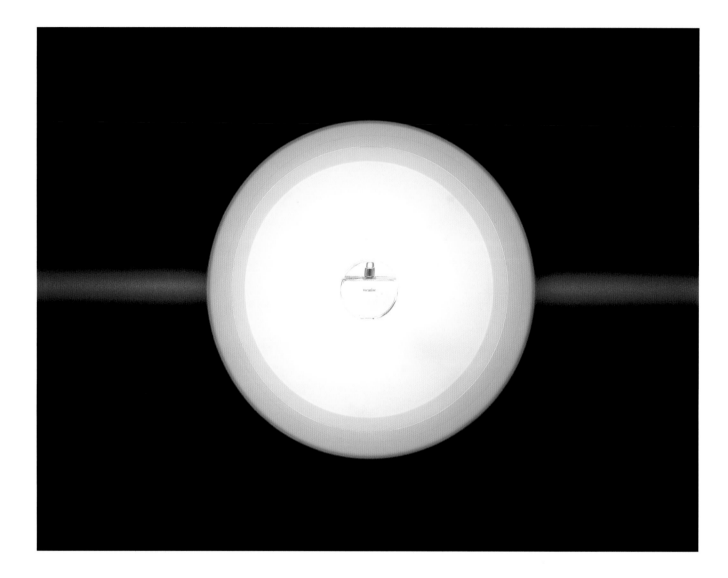

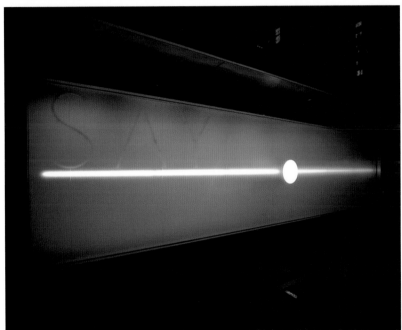

Design Firm: Cyclone
Art Director: Janay Blazejewski /
McCann Erickson, Seattle
Designers, Illustrators:
Traci Daberko, Dennis Clouse
Writer: Jennie Meyer, Reed
Coss / McCann Erickson, Seattle
Production: Sara Lehman
Client: Nanotainment

Design Firm: Cyclone
Art Director: Janay Blazejewski /
McCann Erickson, Seattle
Designers, Illustrators:
Traci Daberko, Dennis Clouse
Writer: Jennie Meyer, Reed
Coss / McCann Erickson, Seattle
Production: Sara Lehman
Client: Nanotainment

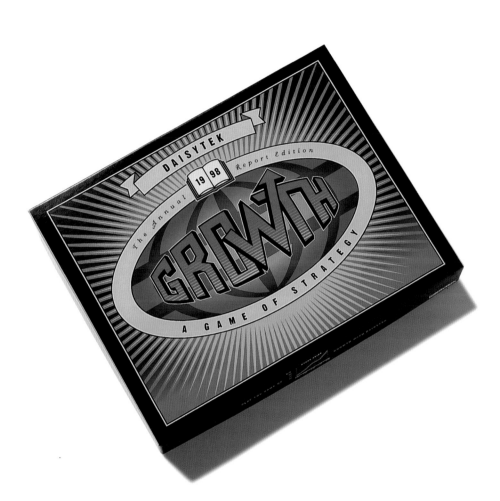

Design Firm:
Rolf Jansson Design
Illustrator:
Rolf Jansson
Client: Vårt Land
Publishing House

(this page)
Design Firm: Burckhardt Studio
Designer, Illustrator:
Marc Burckhardt
Client: Burckhardt Studio

(opposite)
Design Firm: Münk-Illus
Art Director, Illustrator: Siemar Münk
Client: Münk-Illus

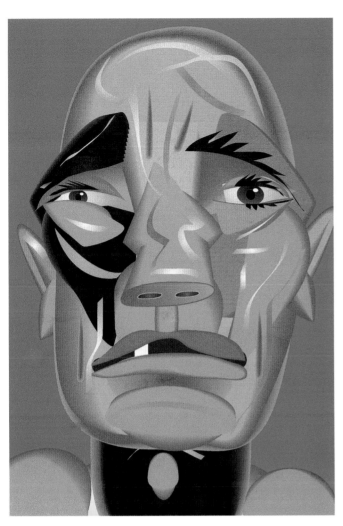
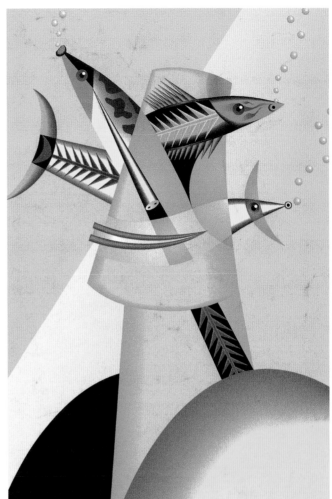

Design Firm: Hendler Inc.
Art Director, Designer, Illustrator:
Sandra Hendler

s.hendler

(opposite)
Illustrator: John Rush
Client: NIPSCO Industries

(this page)
Illustrator: Cathleen Toelke
Client: The Premier Hotel

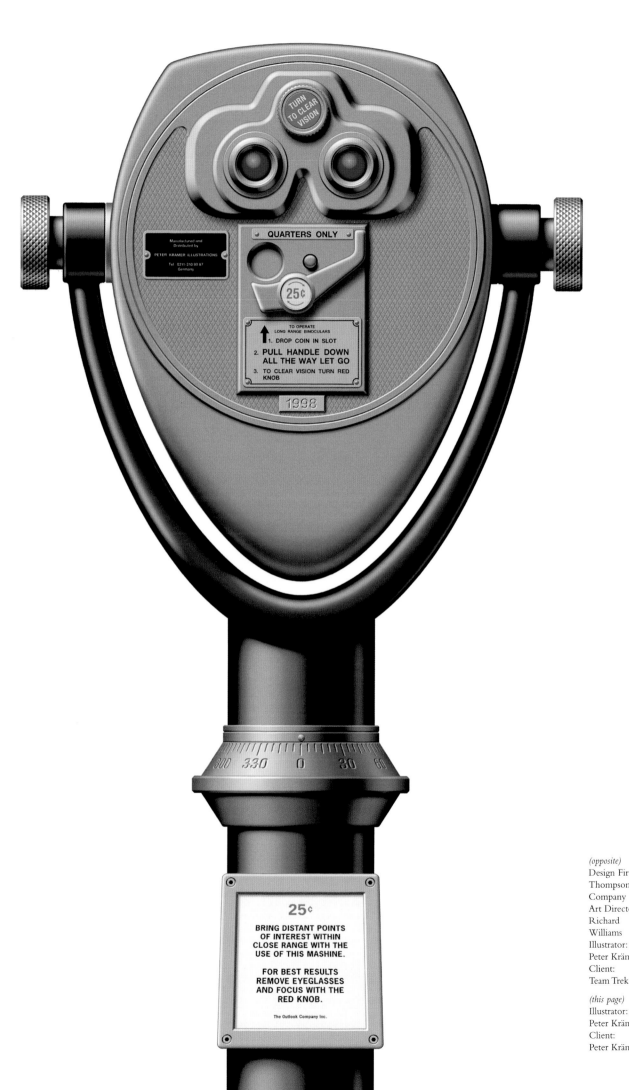

TURN
TO CLEAR
VISION

QUARTERS ONLY

25¢

TO OPERATE
LONG RANGE BINOCULARS
1. DROP COIN IN SLOT
2. PULL HANDLE DOWN
   ALL THE WAY LET GO
3. TO CLEAR VISION TURN RED
   KNOB

1998

Manufactured and
Distributed by
PETER KRÄMER ILLUSTRATIONS
Tel 0211-210 90 87
Germany

300   330   0   30   60

25¢

BRING DISTANT POINTS
OF INTEREST WITHIN
CLOSE RANGE WITH THE
USE OF THIS MASHINE.

FOR BEST RESULTS
REMOVE EYEGLASSES
AND FOCUS WITH THE
RED KNOB.

The Outlook Company Inc.

(opposite)
Design Firm:
Thompson &
Company
Art Director:
Richard
Williams
Illustrator:
Peter Krämer
Client:
Team Trek

(this page)
Illustrator:
Peter Krämer
Client:
Peter Krämer

(this page)
Art Director: Gail Dubov
Illustrator: Cathleen Toelke
Client: Avon Books

(opposite)
Art Director:
Michele Hernandez
Illustrator:
Cathleen Toelke
Client: Scholastic/Literary
Cavalcade

(this page)
Design Firm: Deep Design
Art Director: Edward Jett
Designer,
Illustrator: Philip Shore
Client: Dr. Smith's
Veterinary Collectibles

(opposite)
Design Firm: Sandstrom
Design
Creative Director,
Art Director,
Designer: Steve Sandstrom
Writer: Steve Sandoz.
Client: Filmcore

(opposite)
Design Firm:
Drive Communications
Art Director, Designer:
Michael Graziolo
Photographer: Susan Todd
Client: Archipelago Films

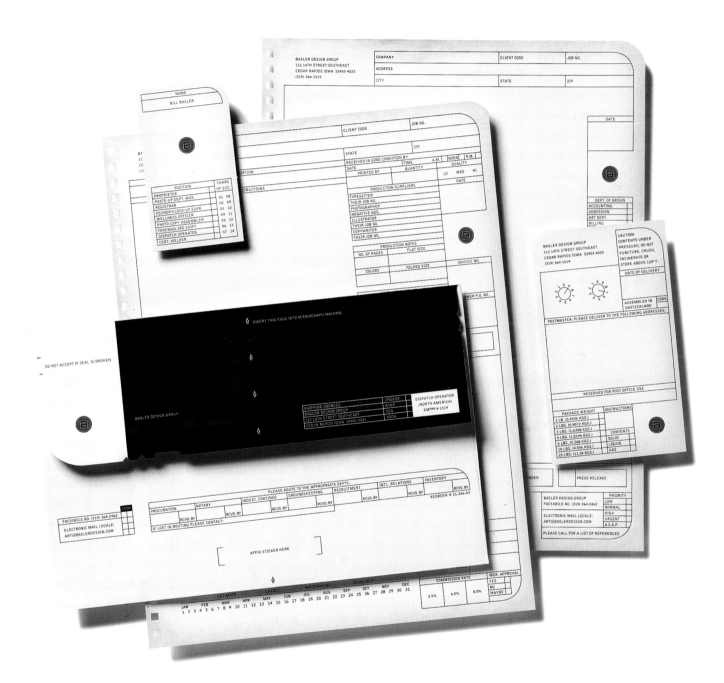

(this page)
Design Firm: Basler
Design Group
Creative Director: Bill Basler
Art Director: Drew Davies
Designers: Bill Basler,
Drew Davies, Bill Bollman
Client: Basler Design Group

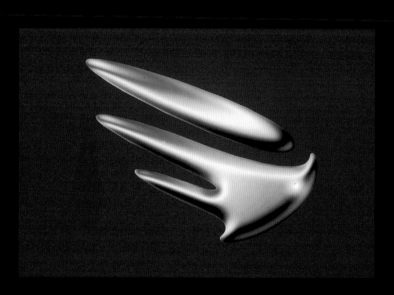

(opposite)
Design Firm:
SDG /
Scandinavian
Design Group
Creative Director:
Gary Swindell
Designer:
Gary Swindell,
Anne Marit
Brenden,
Benedicte Paulsen
Illustrator:
Henning Arnesen
Client:
Braathens

(this page)
Design Firm:
The Rocket
Scientists
Creative Director:
Charl Ritter
Art Director,
Designer,
Illustrator:
Eduard Claassen
Client:
The Rocket
Scientists

(this page, from top)
(1) Design Firm:
Phoenix
Design Works
Creative Director,
Art Director
Designer,
Illustrator:
James M. Skiles
Client: Phoenix
Design Works

(2) Design Firm:
BNA Design Ltd.
Creative Director:
Grenville Main
Art Director,
Designer: Andrew
Sparrow
Illustrator:
Gareth Jensen
Design
Production:
Andrew Sparrow,
Carolyn Cole
Client: Sector 14

(3) Design Firm:
Thom & Dave
Marketing Design
Creative Director:
Thom Holden
Art Director,
Illustrator:
Dave Bell
Designers:
Dave Bell,
Gins Higgins
Client:
Thom & Dave
Marketing Design

(opposite, from top)
(1) Design Firm:
Felix Sockwell
Creative
Designer,
Illustrator:
Felix Sockwell
Client:
Angelika
Film Center

(2) Design Firm:
Ron Kellum Inc.
Designer:
Ron Kellum
Client: Hybrid
Recordings

(3) Design Firm:
Matthias Mencke
(in-house)
Creative Director,
Designer:
Matthias Mencke
Client: Matthias
Mencke

(4) Design Firm:
Realm
Communications
Art Director,
Designer: Steve
McGuffie
Client: TLC
Resort Group /
Ocean Ridge
Resort & Spa

(5) Design Firm:
Vaughn Wedeen
Creative
Creative Director:
Steve Wedeen,
Pamela Chang
Art Director: Steve
Wedeen
Designer:
Pamela Chang
Client: Stockton
Reinsurance

(this page)
Design Firm: David Carter
Design Associates
Creative Director: Lori B. Wilson
Art Director, Designer: Cynthia Carter
Illustrator: Randall Hill
Photographer: Richard Klein
Production: Lynn Pendergrass
Client: Disney Cruise Line

(opposite, from top)
(1) Design Firm: Pentagram Design
Art Director: Michael Gericke
Client: Women's Venture Fund

(2) Design Firm: Mires Design
Creative Director,
Art Director: John Ball
Designer: Deborah Hom. Client: Nike

(3) Design Firm:
David Carter Design Associates
Creative Director: Lori B. Wilson
Art Director: Sharon LeJeune
Designer, Illustrator: Tien Pham
Client: Sun International

(4) Design Firm:
Charles S. Anderson Design Co.

Art Director: Charles Anderson
Designer: Kyle Hames
Client: Sub Zero Advertising

(5) Design Firm:
Matthias Mencke (in-house)
Creative Director, Designer:
Matthias Mencke
Client: Matthias Mencke

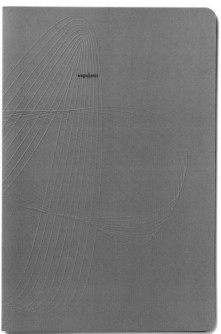

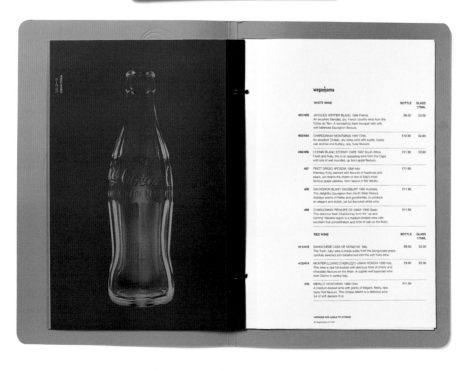

(opposite)
Design Firm: Hirano Studio
Art Director, Designer:
Keiko Hirano
Client: Toshiba EMI Limited

(this page, top and middle)
Design Firm:
Jennifer Sterling Design
Creative Director, Designer,
Illustrator:
Jennifer Sterling
Writer: Deonne Kahler
Client: Bhoss

(this page, bottom)
Design Firm:
Christina Krutz Design
Art Directors: Christina Krutz,
Thomas Sassenbach
Designer: Christina Krutz
Photographer:
Wolf-Dieter Böttcher
Client: BMG Ariola Media
GmbH

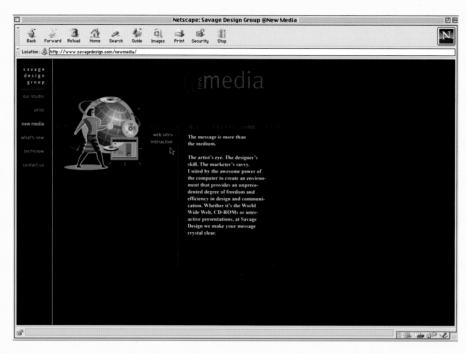

(this page)
Design Firm:
Savage Design
Group
Creative Director:
Paula Savage
Designer: Doug
Hebert
Writer: Savage
Design
Illustrator:
Steven Lyons
Photographer:
Ralph Smith,
Michael Hart
Client:
Savage Design
Group

(opposite)
Design Firm:
Art Center
College
of Design
(in-house)
Creative Director:
Steven Nowlin
Designer:
Francesca
Murphy
Photographer:
Stephen A. Heller
Javascript:
Ben Curtis
Client: Art Center
College
of Design

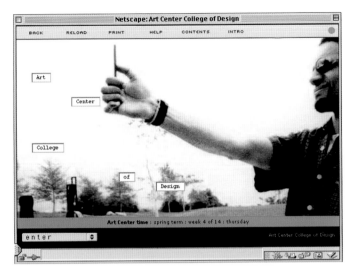

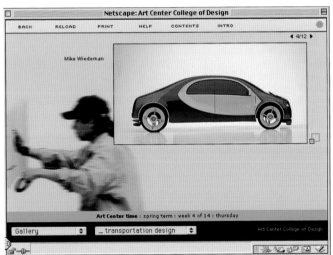

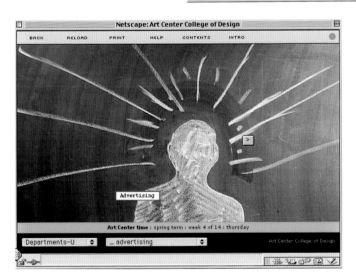

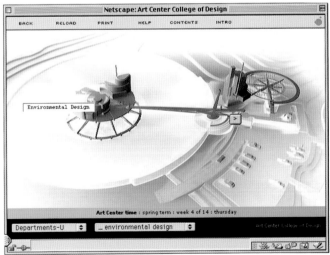

Design Firm:
Caldera Design
Designer:
Caldera Design
Client: Bombardier
Aerospace

Design Firm:
Laughlin / Constable
(Griffin Design)
Creative Director:
Mark Drewek
Art Director, Designer:
Jason Herkent
Writer: John Schaub
Illustrator:
Barbara McAdams
Photographer:
Steve Eliason
Production: Paula Rothe
Client:
Wisconsin Tourism

Design Firm:
Karim Rashid Inc.
Designer:
Karim Rashid
Client: Issey Miyake
Inc., Japan

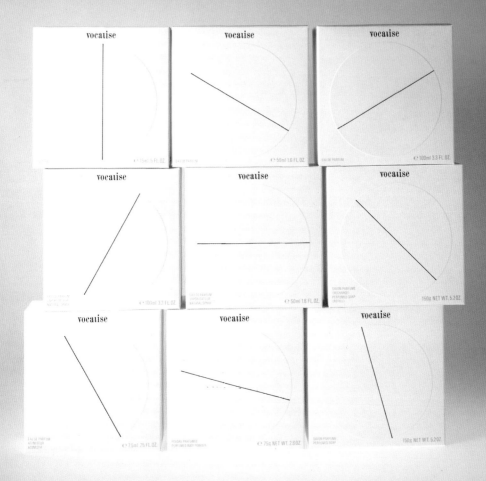

vocalise

EAU DE PARFUM
VAPORISATEUR
NATURAL SPRAY

vocalise

℮ 50ml 1.6 FL.OZ.

(opposite, top)
Design Firm:
Fossil
(in-house)
Creative Director:
Tim Hale
Art Director:
Brad Bollinger
Designer:
Brad Bollinger,
Eric Venegas,
Alicia Cobb
Client: Fossil

(opposite, bottom)
Design Firm:
Fossil
(in-house)
Creative Director,
Art Director:
Tim Hale
Designer:
Stuart Cameron
Client: Fossil

(this page)
Design Firm:
Fossil
(in-house)
Creative Director:
Tim Hale
Art Director:
Stephen Zhang
Designer:
David Eden
Photographer:
Dave McCormick
Client: Fossil

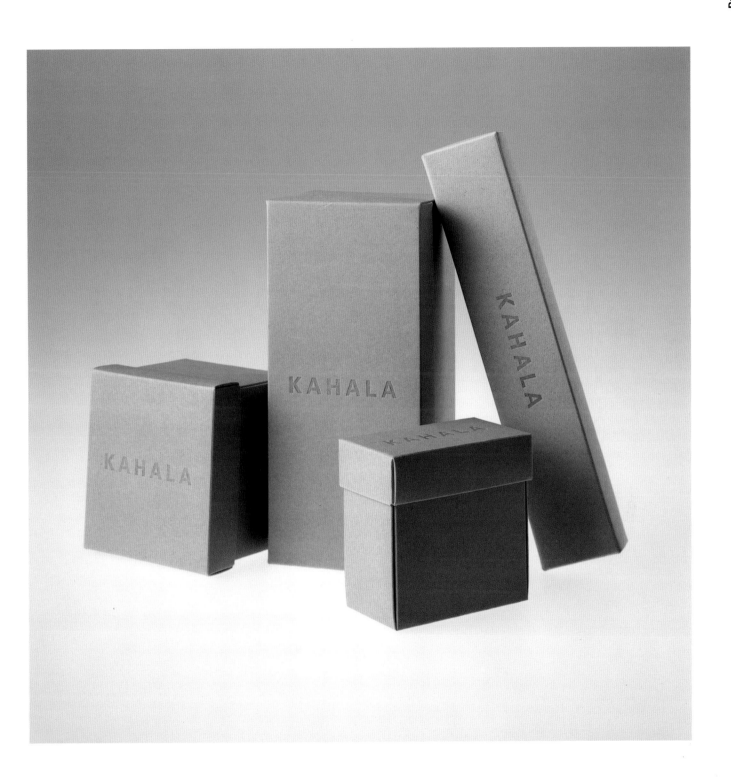

Design Firm: Hornall Anderson
Design Works
Creative Directors, Art Directors:
Lisa Cerveny, Jack Anderson
Designers: Lisa Cerveny, Jack
Anderson, Alan Florsheim,
David Bates, Mike Calkins
Writer: Leatherman Tool Group
Photographer: Condit Studio
Client: Leatherman Tool Group

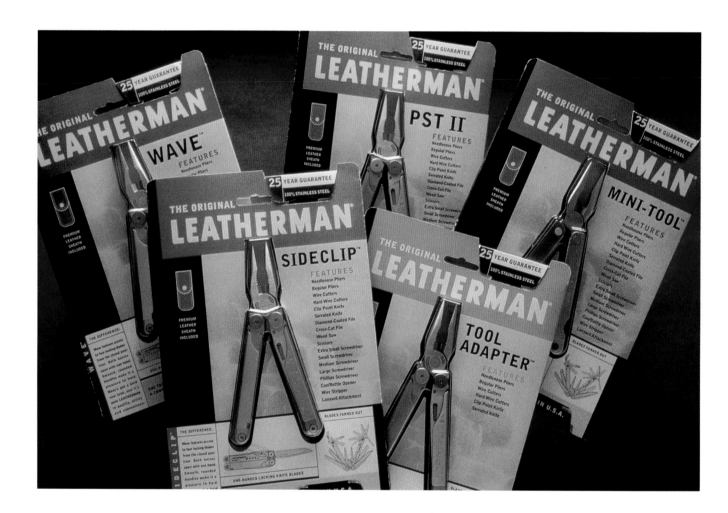

Design Firm: Design Guys
Creative Director, Art Director:
Steven Sikora
Designers: Steven Sikora,
Scott Thares, Gary Patch
Photographer: Jim Erickson
Project Director: Julie Utendorfer
Client: Target Stores

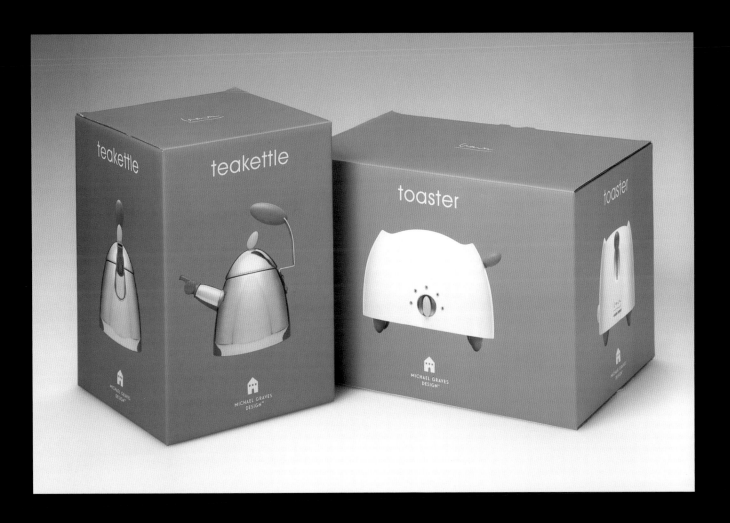

(opposite)
Design Firm: SDG /Scandinavian
Design Group
Designers: Knut Bang, Sven Skaara
Client: The Pure Water Co.

(this page)
Design Firm: Sandstrom Design
Creative Director, Art Director,
Designer: Steve Sandstrom
Writer: Steve Sandoz
Photographers: Mark
Hooper, Steve Sandstrom,
Steve Smith. Client: Tazo

(opposite)
Design Firm: SDG /Scandinavian
Design Group
Designers: Knut Bang, Sven Skaara
Client: The Pure Water Co.

(this page)
Design Firm: Sandstrom Design
Creative Director, Art Director,
Designer: Steve Sandstrom
Writer: Steve Sandoz
Photographers: Mark
Hooper, Steve Sandstrom,
Steve Smith. Client: Tazo

(opposite)
Design Firm: Parachute Design
Designer: Heather Cooley
Advertising Agency:
Clarity Coverdale Fury
Client: Belvedere Vodka and
Millennium Import Co.

(this page)
Design Firm: Packaging Create
Art Director:
Akio Okumura
Designer: Mitsuo Ueno
Client: City of City

(this page)
Design Firm: DFS Group Ltd.
Creative Director: Amy Knapp
Art Director, Designer:
Jane McCampbell
Writers: Lessley Berry,
Sue Garibaldi
Illustrator: Hamagami Carroll
& Associates, Hom²
Illustration, Danny Pelavin,
Tom Nikosey
Photographer: Deborah Jones
Client: The Disney Store

(opposite)
Design Firm: Taku Satoh
Design Office
Creative Director, Art Director,
Designer: Taku Satoh
Client: Lotte Co., Ltd.

Design Firm: SGL Design
Creative Director: Brad
Ghormley
Designer: Peter Jones
Illustrator:
Randy Geske
Photographer:
Rick Gayle
Client: Shamrock Farms

Design Firm: Greteman Group
Creative Director,
Art Director,
Illustrator: Sonia Greteman
Designers: James Strange,
Sonia Greteman
Computer Illustrator: Craig Tomson
Client: Tabacos Gran Columbia

Design Firm: Via
Creative Director: Oscar Fernández
Designers: Oscar Fernández,
Andreas Kranz
Writers: Wendie Wulf,
Kari Lowery
Production Shelly Pomponio
Client: Fraser Papers

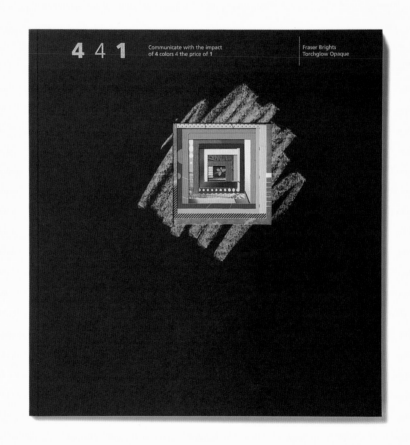

Design Firm: Via
Creative Director: Oscar Fernández
Designers: Oscar Fernández,
Andreas Kranz
Writers: Wendie Wulf,
Kari Lowery
Production Shelly Pomponio
Client: Fraser Papers

Design Firm:
Oliver Kuhlmann
Art Director:
Deanna Kuhlmann
Leavitt
Writer: Mead Coated
Papers (in-house)
Photographer:
David Gill
Client:
Mead Coated Papers

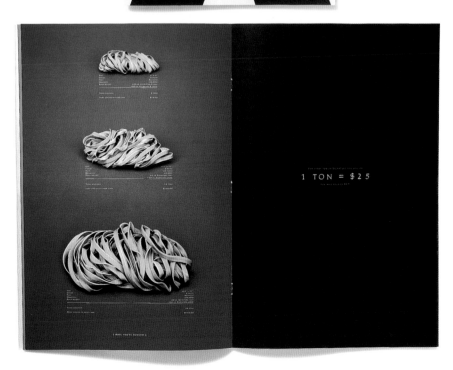

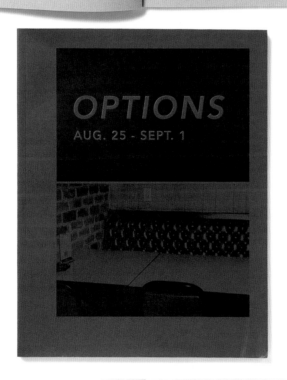

POTLATCH McCoy™

POTLATCH Makers®

POTLATCH Northwest®

POTLATCH

RCMP

POTLATCH McCoy

Potlatch McCoy covers all the bases, with an incredibly ultra bright blue white shade, a choice of popular basis weights, and four versatile finishes – Gloss, Velvet, Silk and Velour. With the character and eye-popping brilliance of a premium sheet and pricing closer to a No. 1, Potlatch McCoy is redefining the paper grading system. In every way, this Plus One paper consistently performs like a champion on press and in the bindery. You'll stand up and cheer when you see the dazzling color reproduction and smooth lay of inks on the sheet. Acid free for archival permanence, Potlatch McCoy will give you finished pieces that you'll proudly hang onto.

COVER PRINTED ON POTLATCH MCCOY GLOSS, 100-POUND COVER   PHOTOGRAPHY BY TERRY HEFFERNAN

POTLATCH Makers

Hard-working and reliable, Makers is a tool that printers often turn to when seeking a quality recycled sheet that can handle high-volume printing jobs economically. With its excellent bulk and opacity, Makers looks and feels substantial. Its balanced white shade assures color fidelity, while its matte-coated finish provides a non-glare surface that enhances readability. Containing a minimum 10% post-consumer fiber, Makers is a practical choice for everyday needs.

COVER PRINTED ON VINTAGE GLOSS, 100-POUND COVER   PHOTOGRAPHY BY TERRY HEFFERNAN

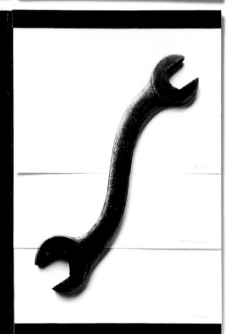

POTLATCH

A recycled paper that printers love for its practicality and performance, Northwest is now offered in a brighter blue-white shade. Containing a minimum 10% post-consumer recycled waste, this versatile coated sheet comes in both Gloss and Dull finishes and a full range of basis weights. Its exclusive blade-coated surface is designed to capture the full spectrum of colors accurately and to reproduce images in crisp detail. Always up to the challenge, Northwest is the paper that printers turn to when they need to get the job done.

COVER PRINTED ON VINTAGE GLOSS, 100-POUND COVER   PHOTOGRAPHY BY TERRY HEFFERNAN

Design Firm:
The Rocket Scientists
Creative Director: Charl Ritter
Designer, Illustrator,
Writer: Eduard Claassen
Client: Sappi Fine Papers

Design Firm:
The Rocket Scientists
Creative Director: Charl Ritter
Designer, Illustrator,
Writer: Eduard Claassen
Client: Sappi Fine Papers

Council, Design Dept.
Design Director: Mathew Leung
Designers: Irwin Wong,
Peter Lau, Shirley Fung
Client: Hong Kong
Trade Development Council

Think about the Contacts!

Our computerised trade enquiry service helps you find the right supplier, buyer or agent among **600,000 contacts**

香港貿易發展局
Hong Kong Trade Development Council

(this page)
Design Firm: Hägersten
Art Director, Designer:
Dan Jonsson. Client: Galleri Grå

(opposite)
Design Firm: Art Force
Creative Director: Attila Simon
Art Director, Designer,
Illustrator: Tamás Veress
Client: Art Force Studio

GALLERI GRÅ   Sturegat. 44 Stockholm

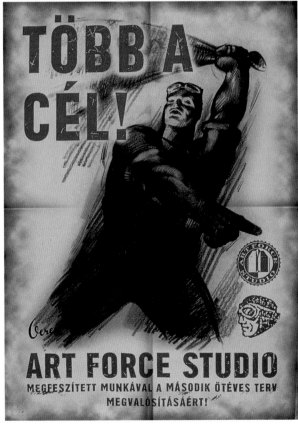

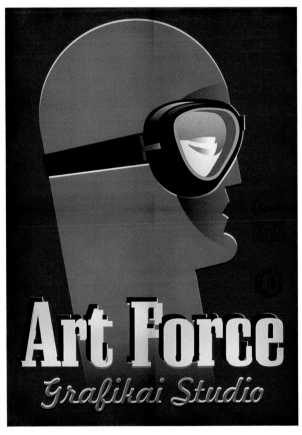

(this page)
Design Firm: The Pushpin Group Inc.
Designer: Seymour Chwast
Producer: Cora Weiss
Client: The Hague: Appeal For Peace

(opposite)
Art Director, Designer, Photographer:
Gabriele Strijewski
Client: Fotografie Forum Frankfurt

Gabriele Strijewski Anfangs ging ich barfuß durch das Gras zum Fluß. 22. März - 27. April 1997. **Fotografie Forum Frankfurt** Leinwandhaus 1. Stock, Weckmarkt 17. Di - Fr 11 - 18, Mi 11 - 20, Sa/So 11 - 17. Mo geschlossen.

Finnish Cultural Posters designed by
Tapani Aartomaa and Kari Piippo

Finnish Institute at Athens
Zitrou 16, Makrigianni
Tel. 9221 152
Open Monday – Friday 9 a.m. – 2 p.m.
Saturday – Sunday 11 a.m. – 2 p.m.
25th September – 16th October

(opposite)
Design Firm: Studio Aartomaa Oy
Creative Director, Art Director:
Tapani Aartomaa
Writer, Typographer: Kari Piippo
Photographer: Teemu Töyrylä
Client: Finnish Institute at Athens

Ein farbiges Jahr bei Bösch Siebdruck AG Stans/Luzern

(this page)
Design Firm: Niklaus Troxler Design
Creative Director, Art Director,
Designer, Illustrator: Niklaus Troxler
Client: Boesch Silkscreen Co.

Design Firm: Viva Dolan
Communications & Design
Designer: Frank Viva
Photographer: Ron Baxter Smith
Client: The Advertising
and Design Club of Canada

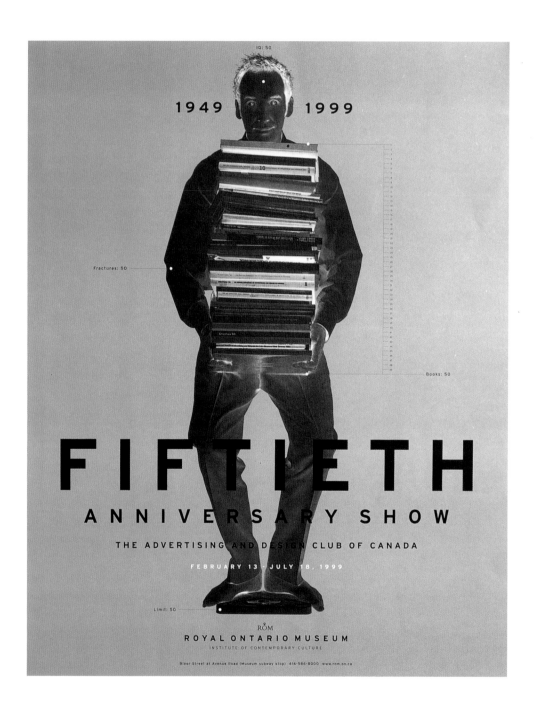

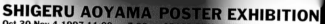

SHIGERU AOYAMA POSTER EXHIBITION
Oct.30-Nov.4,1997 11:00am-7:00pm SPACE PRISM DESIGNERS GALLERY
The DESIGN NAGOYA Design Competition Grand Prize Memorial Exhibition

S

A

SHIGERU AOYAMA POSTER EXHIBITION
Oct.30-Nov.4,1997 11:00am-7:00pm SPACE PRISM DESIGNERS GALLERY
The DESIGN NAGOYA Design Competition Grand Prize Memorial Exhibition

Design Firm: Aoyama
Design Office
Creative Director, Art Director,
Designer, Illustrator:
Shigeru Aoyama
Client: Design Nagoya
Working Committee

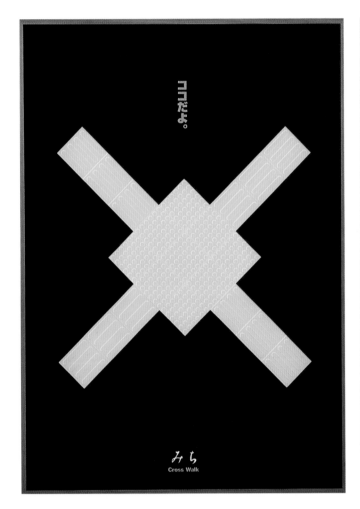

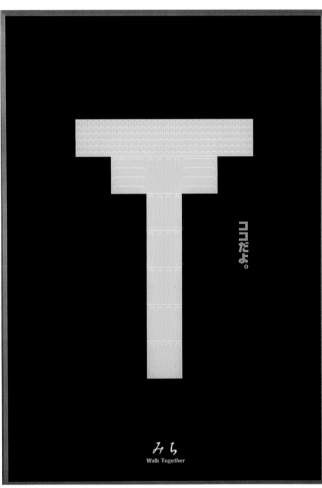

Design Firm: Rempen & Partner:
Das Design Büro
Creative Director:
Stefan Baggen
Art Director: Helen Hacker
Client: Kunsthalle Düsseldorf

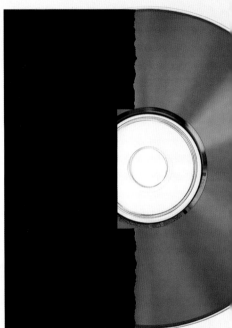

KAN. TAI - KEUNG

KA

AMERICAN INSTITUTE OF ARCHITECTS NEW YORK CHAPTER HERITAGE BALL! NOVEMBER 19, 1998

HONORING LEWIS DAVIS, SAMUEL BRODY AND RICHARD RAVITCH PIERRE HOTEL, NEW YORK CITY

1937

1997

oCTObER

/18

CONCEPT

CONCEPT / .CAC / .8th. ANNUAL .DESIGN .LECTURE .SYMPOSIUM

1.

2.

3.

4.

sPEAKERS

date   year   location
        9:      S.F. campus
oct.
    1 2 3 4 5 6 7 8 9 10 11 12 13 14 15 16 17 18 (A) symposium

9.00 a.m.–4.00 P.M.

(opposite)
Design Firm: Jennifer Sterling Design
Creative Director, Art Director,
Designer: Jennifer Sterling
Client: California College of Arts
and Crafts

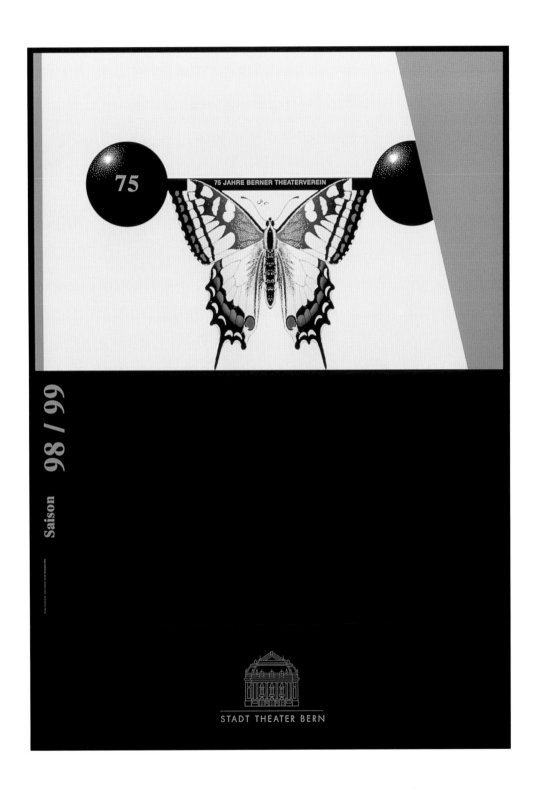

(this page)
Design Firm: Pentagram Design Inc.
Art Director, Designer:
John Klotnia. Client: AIGA

Designers: Josh Goldfarb, Simon Yan, on Lindholm

Client: Herbst Lazar Bell

Comments: Zuzu's Petals is a docking tation for various small electronics and omputer equipment. Each "petal" s a different tool, palm-sized for porta- can be worn. Zuzu sits near a window just like a plant—this way it can access satellite networks and recharge its solar power cells. Each leaf has a unique function. The Personal Digital Assistant unit contatins an integrated stylus, fans out to create a screen, can be voice programmable, and acts as an Internet interface. The Digital Image Capture Device and the Digital Audio Assistant store images and sound; the Digital Dirt located in the base is made of modules of energy storage area. (Zuzu can be repotted to upgrade the capabilities.)

Design Firm: Portfolio Center
Creative Director:
Hank Richardson
Designer: Lenoir Love

Design Firm: Portfolio Center
Creative Director:
Hank Richardson
Designer: Scott McBride

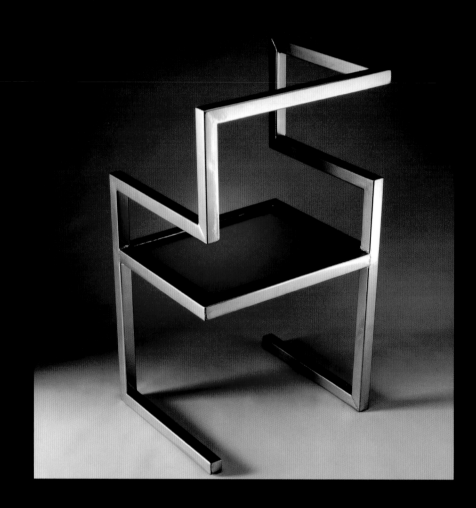

(opposite)
Design Firm: Portfolio Center
Creative Director: Hank Richardson
Designer: Eric Miller

(this page)
Design Firm: Kilter (in-house)
Creative Director: Cynthia Knox
Designers: Tim Schumann, David
Richardson, Jamie Parker
Client: Kilter Industries

Design Firm: Taku Satoh
Design Office
Creative Director,
Art Director, Designer:
Taku Satoh
Client: Japan Tupperware

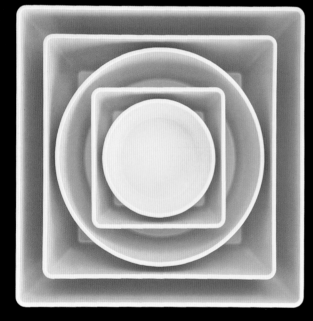
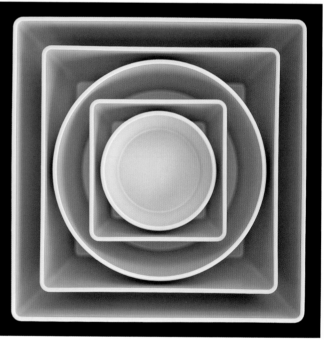

Design Firm:
Herbst Lazar Bell
Designers:
Greg Holderfield,
Josh Goldfarb
Client: GBC

Design Firm:
Herbst Lazar Bell
Designers: Mark Dziersk,
Albert Chelis
Client: Tenex

Design Firm: Vaughn Wedeen Creative
Creative Directors:
Foster Hurley, Rick Vaughn
Art Directors: Rick Vaughn, Steve Wedeen.

Designer: Rick Vaughn
Writer: Foster Hurley
Production: Kristine Dusing
Client: Vaughn Wedeen Creative

Design Firm: Vaughn Wedeen Creative
Creative Directors:
Foster Hurley, Rick Vaughn
Art Directors: Rick Vaughn, Steve Wedeen.

Designer: Rick Vaughn
Writer: Foster Hurley
Production: Kristine Dusing
Client: Vaughn Wedeen Creative

Design Firm:
Zimmermann Crowe Design
Creative Director: Rob Smiley
Art Director: Dennis Crowe
Designer: Doug Becker
Photographer: Jock McDonald
Fabrication: Color Bar
Client: Levi Strauss & Co.

David Gauger
Art Director: Robert Ankers
Designers: Robert Ankers,
David Gauger
Client: Gauger & Silva Associates

Design Firm: Seasonal Specialties
In-House Creative
Creative Director: Barbara J. Roth
Art Director: Lisa Milan
Designers: Barbara J. Roth, Lisa Milan
Photographer: Drew Trampe
Design Production: Deborah Lee,
Rene Demel
Desktop Specialists: Michelle Loch,
Sharon Wilson, Katrina Snow
Client: Seasonal Specialties LLC

(this page)
Design Firm: Demner Merlicek
& Bergmann
Creative Directors:
Mariusz Jan
Demner, Stephan Klein
Art Director: Bernhard Grafl
Writers: Helge Haberzettl,
Stephan Klein
Client: Demner Merlicek
& Bergmann

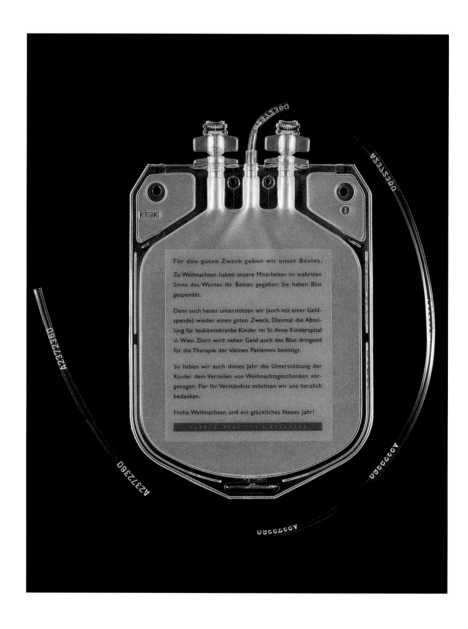

(opposite)
Design Firm: NBBJ Graphic Design
Designers: Bob Boulware,
Billy Chen, Paul Gillis, Ryan Wilkerson
Client: NBBJ Marketing

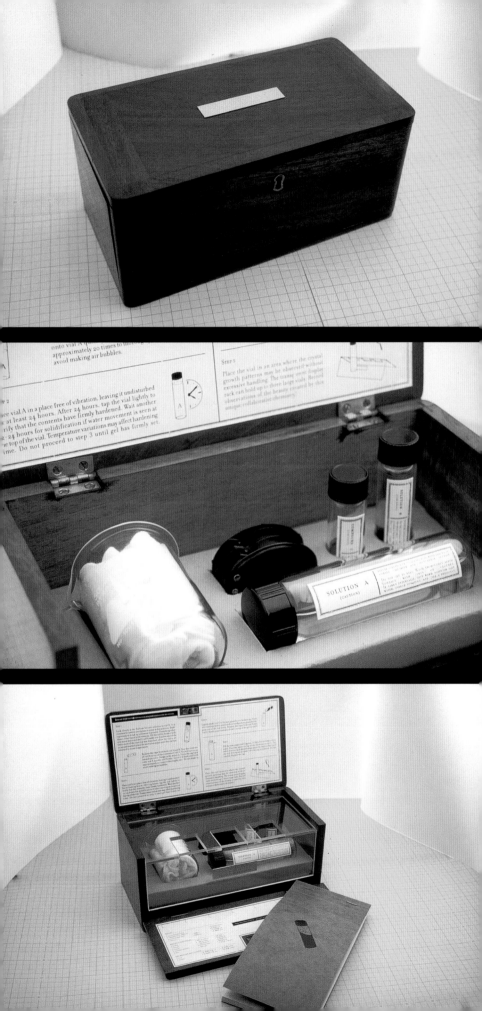

(this page)
Design Firm: SGL Design
Creative Director,
Designer: Art Lofgreen
Client: Pierce
Arrow Lithographers

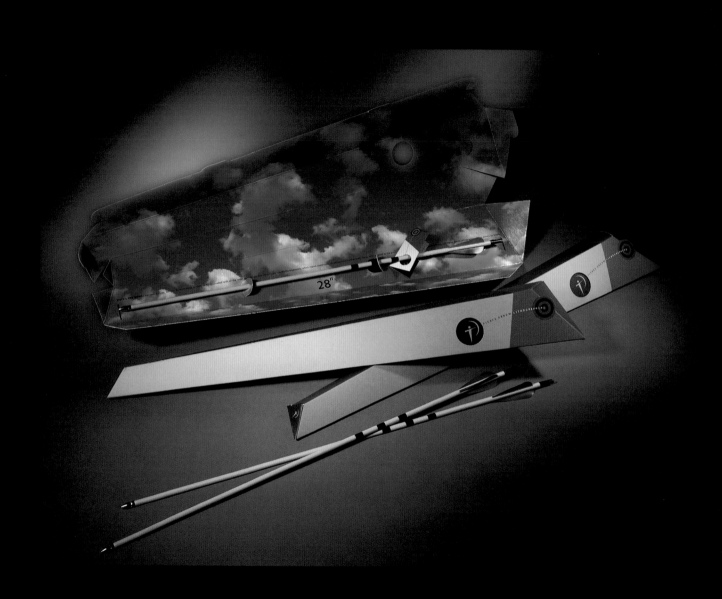

(opposite)
Design Firm: squid design
Designers: Fabian Schmid,
Heather Lafleur
Writers: Heather Lafleur,
Petila Schmid-Guyer
Photographer: Photodisc
Client: squid design

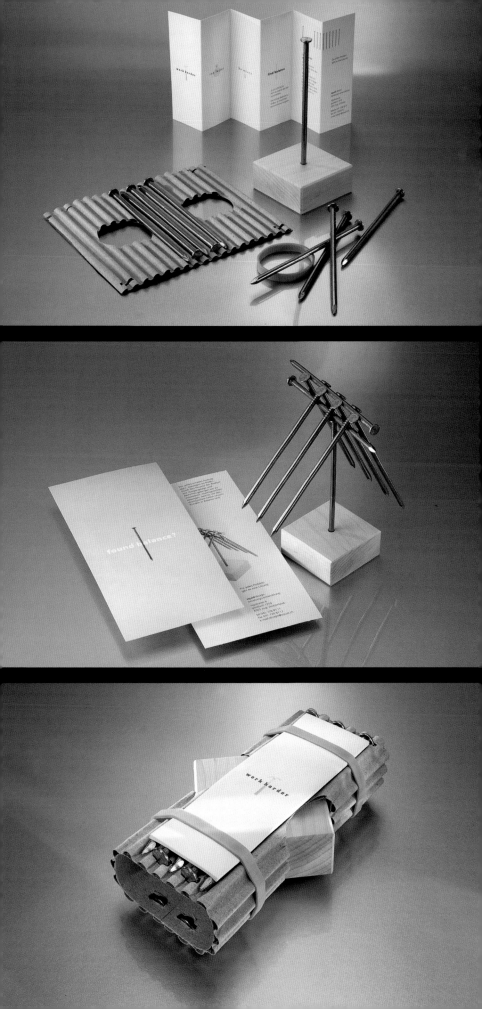

Design Firm: Package
Land Co. Ltd.
Creative Director, Art Director,
Designer: Yasuo Tanaka
Client: Package Land Co. Ltd.

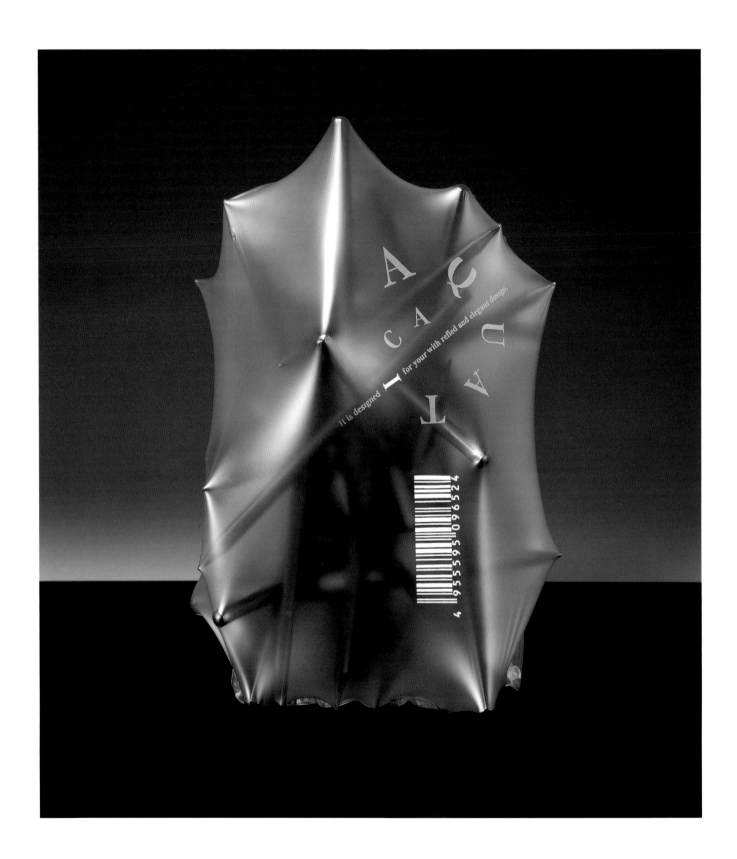

Design Firm: Package
Land Co. Ltd.
Creative Director, Art Director,
Designer: Yasuo Tanaka
Client: Package Land Co. Ltd.

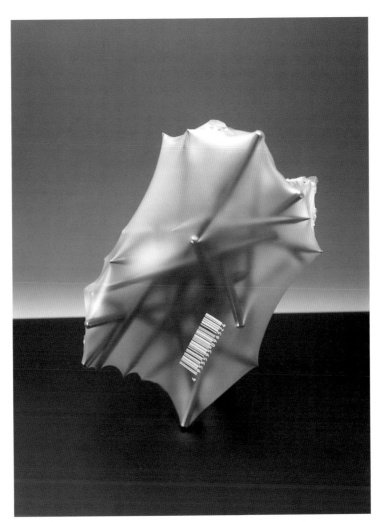

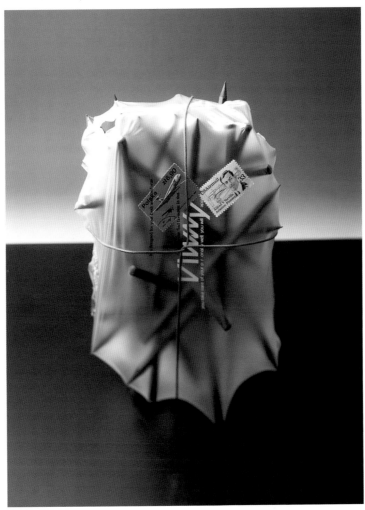

FIRST DAY OF ISSUE

Fine Arts Engraving. Putting our stamp on Washington.

Design Firm: Art Force Studio
Creative Director: Attila Simon
Art Director, Designer, Illustrator:
Tamás Veress
Client: Art Force Studio

(this page)
Design Firm: Drive Communications
Art Director: Michael Graziolo
Designers: Michael Graziolo,
Frank Kierna. Client: Thinc Inc.

(opposite)
Design Firm: Triad Inc.
Creative Directors:
Michael Hinshaw, Gregg Atwood
Art Director, Writer: Michael Hinshaw
Designers: Michael Dambrowski,
Diana Kollanyi. Client: Triad Inc.

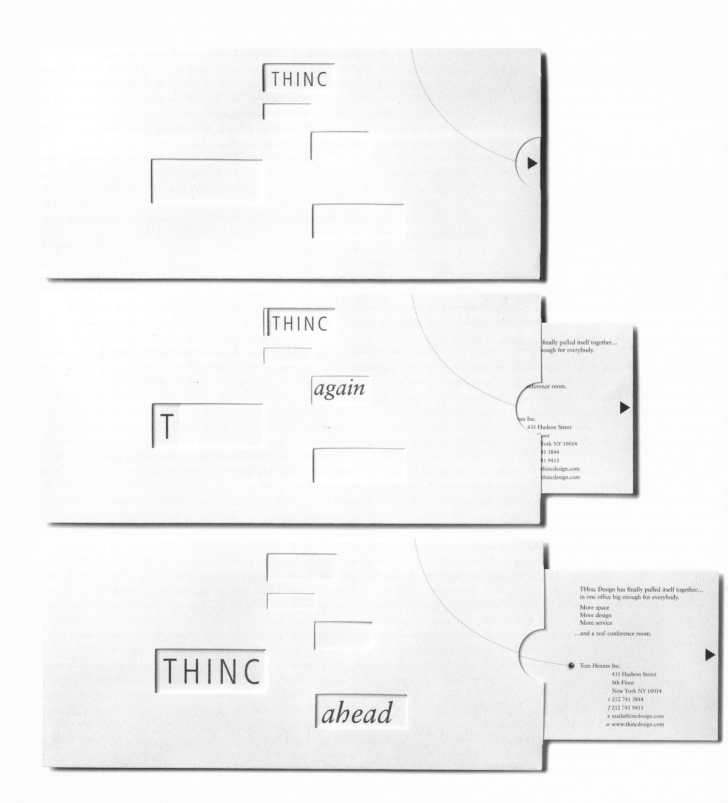

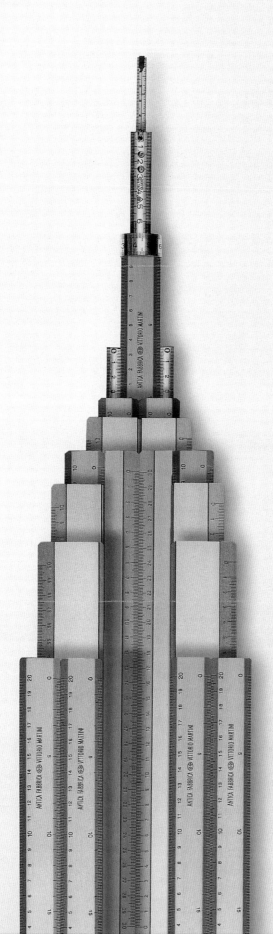

(opposite)
Design Firm:
Mires Design
Creative Director
Art Director:
José A. Serrano
Designer:
Jeff Samaripa
Illustrator:
Miguel Perez
Photographer:
David Deahl
Client: Big Deah

(this page)
Design Firm: Are
Strategic Design
Creative Director
Writer: Antonio
Romano
Art Director:
Stefano Aureu
Designer:
Niccolo Desii
Illustrator:
Francesca Monto
Photographer:
Giuseppe Fadda
Client: Area
Strategic Design

(this page)
Design Firm: The Rocket Scientists
Creative Director: Charl Ritter
Art Director, Designer, Writer,
Illustrator: Eduard Claassen
Client: The Rocket Scientists

(opposite)
Design Firm: The Rocket Scientists
Creative Director: Eduard Claassen
Art Director, Designer: Charl Ritter
Writer: Hennie Reynders
Client: The University of Pretoria

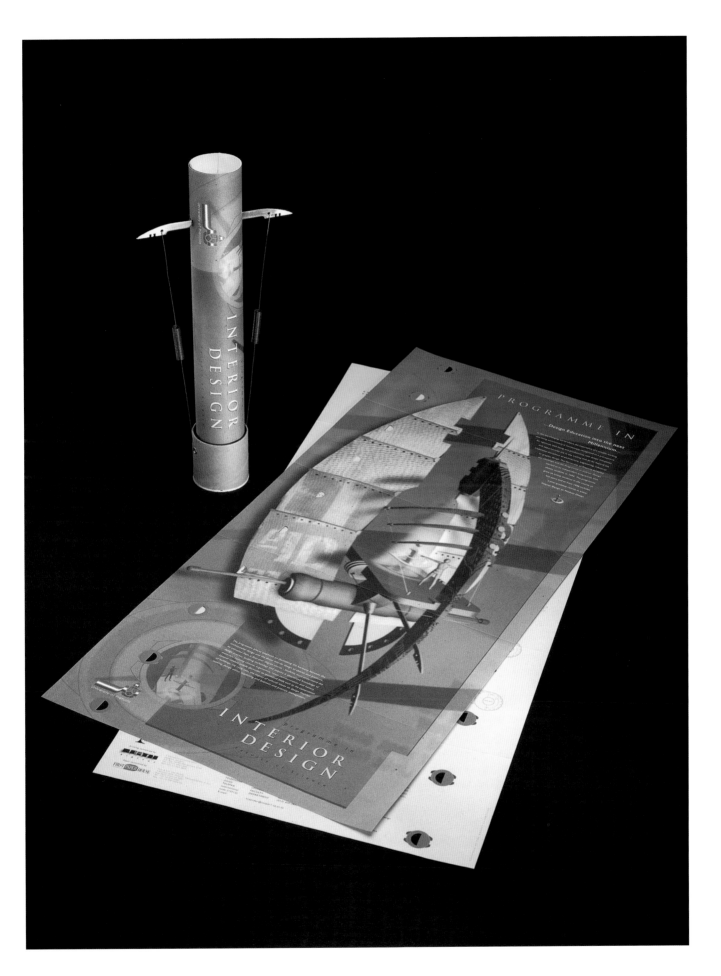

Design Firm: Package
Land Co. Ltd.
Creative Director, Art Director,
Designer: Yasuo Tanaka
Client: Package Land Co. Ltd.

Design Firm: Package
Land Co. Ltd.
Creative Director, Art Director,
Designer: Yasuo Tanaka
Client: Package Land Co. Ltd.

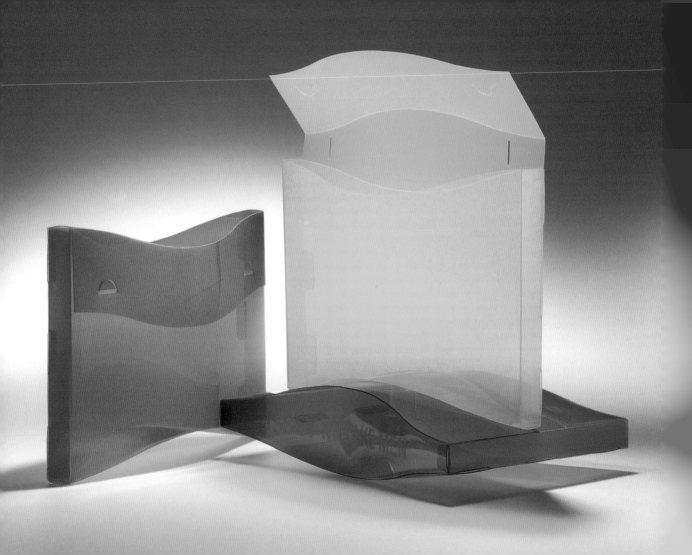

Design Firm: Package
Land Co. Ltd.
Creative Director,
Art Director,
Designer: Yasuo Tanaka
Client: Package Land
Co. Ltd.

Design Firm: Package
Land Co. Ltd.
Creative Director,
Art Director,
Designer: Yasuo Tanaka
Client: Package Land
Co. Ltd.

Design Firm:
Packaging Create
Art Director:
Akio Okumura
Designer: Zhao Hui
Client: Musa

Design Firm: Real Design
Creative Director,
Art Director: Margot Perman
Designer: Catharine Woodman
Photographer: David Heald
Project Directors:
Karen Meyerhoff
(Guggenheim New York), Alicia
Martinez (Guggenheim Bilbao)
Client: Guggenheim Museum
Bilbao

Design Firm:
Zimmermann Crowe Design
Creative Director:
Rob Smiley
Art Director: Dennis Crowe
Designers: Michelle Benzer,
Dennis Crowe
Photographer: Jock McDonald
Typographers:
Jeremy Mende, Laura Scott
Client: Levi Strauss & Co.

Design Firm:
Kim Baer Design Associates
Creative Director,
Art Director: Kim Baer
Designer: Barbara Cooper
Client: Getty
Conservation Institute

(this page)
Design Firm: Kari Piippo Oy
Art Director, Designer:
Kari Piippo
Photographers: Gero Mylius,
Timo Kauppila, Juha Reunanen,
Marco Melander
Client: Suomen Posti Oy

(opposite)
Design Firm: Graphic Design
Art Director, Designer:
Ingo Wulff
Client: Bundesministerium
der Finanzen

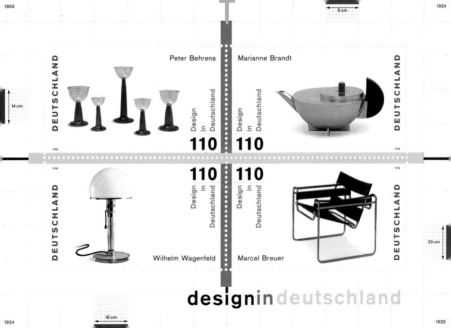

designindeutschland

SAULT STE. MARIE CANAL
CANAL DE SAULT STE. MARIE

PORT CARLING LOCK
ÉCLUSE DE PORT CARLING

TRENT-SEVERN WATERWAY
VOIE NAVIGABLE TRENT-SEVERN

ST. OURS CANAL
CANAL DE SAINT-OURS

LACHINE CANAL
CANAL DE LACHINE

ST. PETERS CANAL
CANAL DE ST. PETERS

RIDEAU CANAL
CANAL RIDEAU

CHAMBLY CANAL
CANAL DE CHAMBLY

ST. PETERS CANAL
CANAL DE ST. PETERS

ST. OURS CANAL
CANAL DE SAINT-OURS

PORT CARLING LOCK
ÉCLUSE DE PORT CARLING

RIDEAU CANAL
CANAL RIDEAU

TRENT-SEVERN WATERWAY
VOIE NAVIGABLE TRENT-SEVERN

CHAMBLY CANAL
CANAL DE CHAMBLY

LACHINE CANAL
CANAL DE LACHINE

TRENT-SEVERN WATERWAY
VOIE NAVIGABLE TRENT-SEVERN

SAULT STE. MARIE CANAL
CANAL DE SAULT STE. MARIE

CANADA CANADA CANADA CANADA CANADA CANADA CANADA CANADA CANADA CANADA

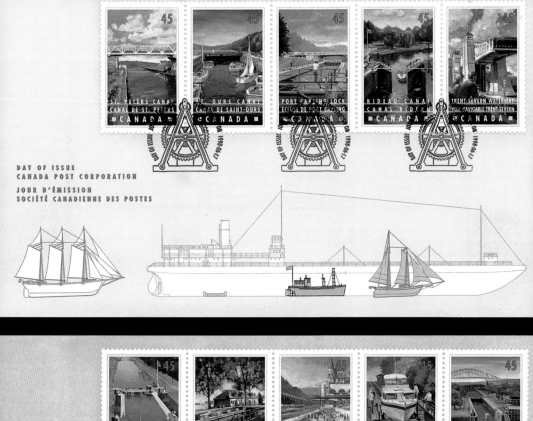

DAY OF ISSUE
CANADA POST CORPORATION

JOUR D'ÉMISSION
SOCIÉTÉ CANADIENNE DES POSTES

DAY OF ISSUE
CANADA POST CORPORATION

JOUR D'ÉMISSION
SOCIÉTÉ CANADIENNE DES POSTES

PORTUGAL 140.

250 Anos da Indústria Vidreira na Marinha Grande

Design : João Machado

Imp : Lito Maia 98

PORTUGAL 100.

250 Anos da Indústria Vidreira na Marinha Grande

Design : João Machado

Imp : Lito Maia 98

18 73

FRÍMERKIÐ 125 ÁRA

35 KRÓNUR

ISLAND

19 98

10,000 donors give blood every day NHS

20

1,700,000 prescriptions dispensed every day NHS

26

2,000 babies delivered every day NHS

43

130,000 hospital outpatients seen every day NHS

63

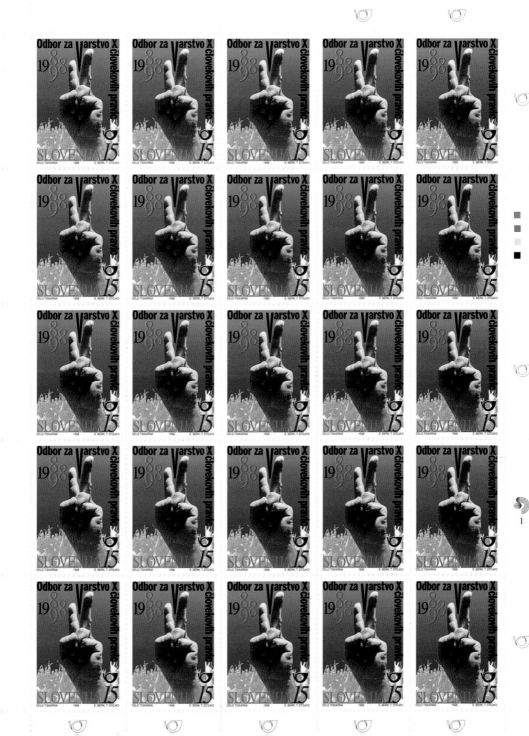

Design Firm: U.S. Postal Service
Creative Director:
Terry McCaffrey
Art Director, Designer:
Derry Noyes
Photographer: Phil Channing
Client: U.S. Postal Service

(opposite)
Design Firm: Phoenix Design Works
Creative Director,
Art Director: James M. Skiles
Designers, Illustrators:
James M. Skiles, Rod Ollerenshaw
Client: Phoenix Design Works

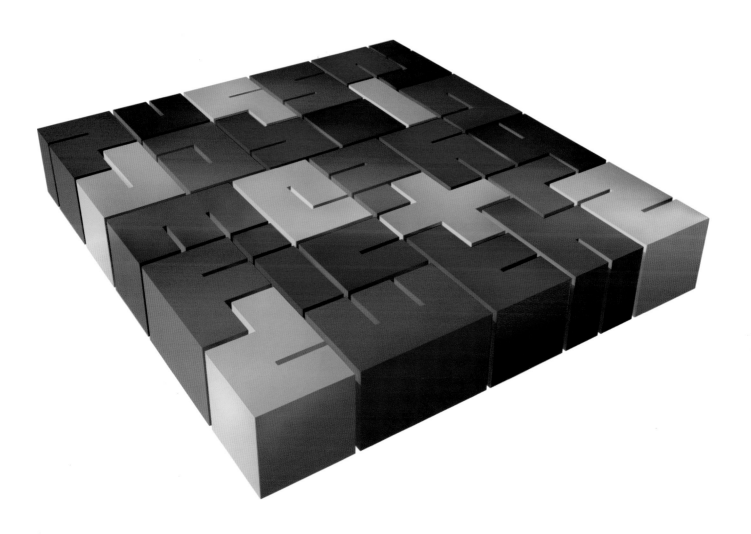

(this page)
Art Director, Designer,
Illustrator: Péter Vajda
Typeface: Puzzle Typeface
Client: Alternativ Studio

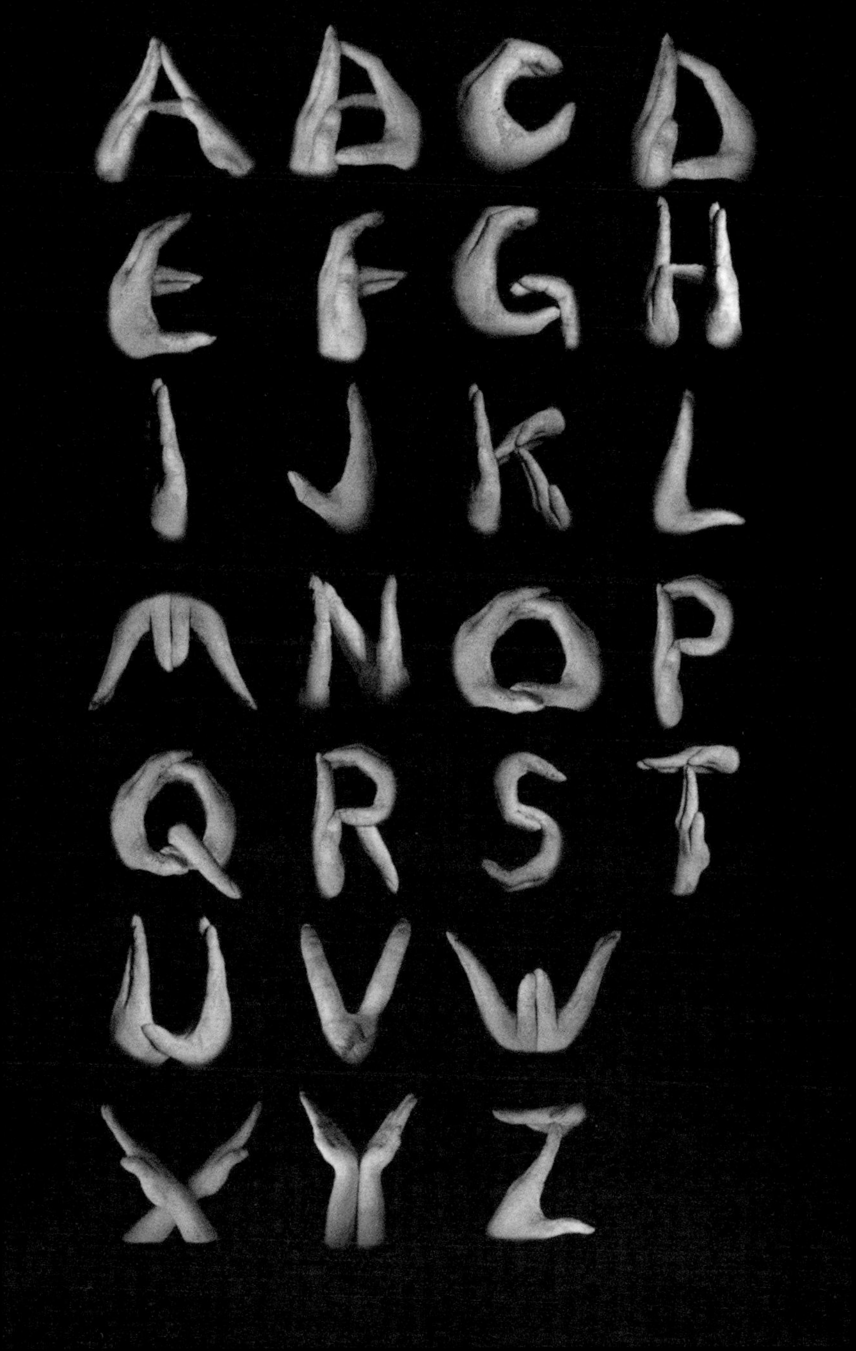
ABCD
EFGH
IJKL
MNOP
QRST
UVW
XYZ

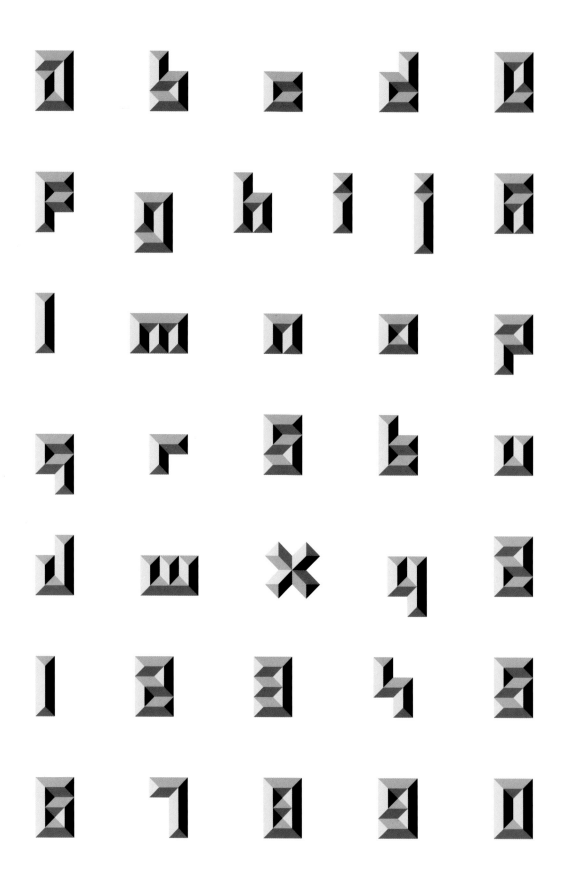

IndexVerzeichnisseIndex

Creative Directors Art Directors Designers

Photographers Illustrators

Design Firms Agencies

Copywriters

Clients

Graphis Books Promotion

Graphis321

Graphis321

Ikko Tanaka
Big Bang
Craig McDean
Rico Lins
David Levine
Albert Watson
David Tang

Order Form

We're introducing a great way to reward Graphis magazine readers: If you subscribe to Graphis, you'll qualify for a 40% discount on our books. If you subscribe and place a Standing Order, you'll get a 50% discount on our books. A Standing Order means we'll reserve your selected Graphis Annual or Series title(s) at press, and ship it to you at 50% discount. With a Standing Order for Design Annual 1999, for example, you'll receive this title at half off, and each coming year, we'll send you the newest Design Annual at this low price — an ideal way for the professional to keep informed, year after year. In addition to the titles here, we carry books in all communication disciplines, so call if there's another title we can get for you. Thank you for supporting Graphis.

Book title	Order No.	Retail	40% off Discount	standing order 50% off	Quantity	Totals
Advertising Annual 1999	1500	☐ $70.00	☐ $42.00	☐ $35.00		
Annual Reports 6 (s)	1550	☐ $70.00	☐ $42.00	☐ $35.00		
Apple Design	1259	☐ $45.00	☐ $27.00	N/A		
Black & White Blues	4710	☐ $40.00	☐ $24.00	N/A		
Book Design 2 (s)	1453	☐ $70.00	☐ $42.00	☐ $35.00		
Brochures 3 (s)	1496	☐ $70.00	☐ $42.00	☐ $35.00		
Corporate Identity 3 (s)	1437	☐ $70.00	☐ $42.00	☐ $35.00		
Digital Photo 1 (s)	1593	☐ $70.00	☐ $42.00	☐ $35.00		
Ferenc Berko	1445	☐ $60.00	☐ $36.00	N/A		
Information Architects	1380	☐ $35.00	☐ $21.00	N/A		
Interactive Design 1 (s)	1631	☐ $70.00	☐ $42.00	☐ $35.00		
Letterhead 4 (s)	1577	☐ $70.00	☐ $42.00	☐ $35.00		
Logo Design 4 (s)	1585	☐ $60.00	☐ $36.00	☐ $30.00		
New Talent Design Annual 1999	1607	☐ $60.00	☐ $36.00	☐ $30.00		
Nudes 1	212	☐ $50.00	☐ $30.00	N/A		
Photo Annual 1998	1461	☐ $70.00	☐ $42.00	☐ $35.00		
Pool Light	1470	☐ $70.00	☐ $42.00	N/A		
Poster Annual 1999	1623	☐ $70.00	☐ $42.00	☐ $35.00		
Product Design 2 (s)	1330	☐ $70.00	☐ $42.00	☐ $35.00		
Promotion Design 1 (s)	1615	☐ $70.00	☐ $42.00	☐ $35.00		
T-Shirt Design 2 (s)	1402	☐ $60.00	☐ $36.00	☐ $30.00		
Typography 2	1267	☐ $70.00	☐ $42.00	☐ $35.00		
Walter Iooss	1569	☐ $60.00	☐ $36.00	N/A		
World Trademarks	1070	☐ $250.00	☐ $150.00	N/A		

Shipping & handling per book, US $7.00, Canada $15.00, International $20.00.

New York State shipments add 8.25% tax.

Standing Orders I understand I am committing to the selected annuals and/or series and will be automatically charged for each new volume in forthcoming years, at 50% off. I must call and cancel my order when I am no longer interested in purchasing the book. (To honor your standing order discount you must sign below.)

_____

Signature _____ Date _____

Graphis magazine					
☐ One year subscription	USA $90	Canada $125	Int'l $125		
☐ Two year subscription	USA $165	Canada $235	Int'l $235		
☐ One year student*	USA $65	Canada $90	Int'l $90		
☐ Single or Back Issues (per)	USA $24	Canada $28	Int'l $28		

*All students must mail a copy of student ID along with the order form.

(s) = series (published every 2-4 years)

Name	☐ American Express ☐ Visa ☐ Mastercard ☐ Check
Company	
Address	Card #
City State Zip	Expiration
Daytime phone	Card holder's signature

Send this order form (or copy) and make check payable to Graphis Inc. For even faster turn-around service, or if you have any questions about subscribing, call us at the following numbers: in the US (800) 209. 4234; outside the US (212) 532. 9387 ext. 242 or 240; fax (212) 696. 4242. Mailing address: Graphis, 141 Lexington Avenue, New York, New York 10016-8193. Order Graphis on the Web from anywhere in the world: <www.graphis.com>.